The Twenty-Four Carat Buddha and Other Fables

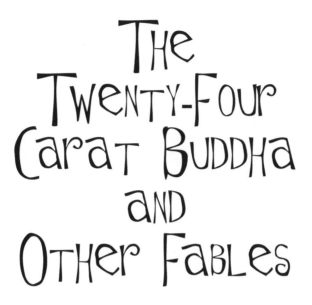

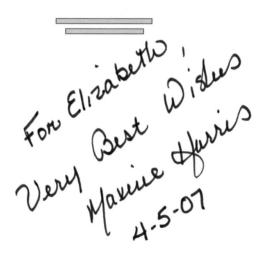

For Elizabeth !
Very Best Wishes
Maxine Harris
4-5-07

All Royalties Benefit Community Connections
Empowerment Center for Abused Women

The Twenty-Four Carat Buddha and Other Fables

Stories of Self-Discovery

by Maxine Harris

with Illustrations by
Tracey Hedrick Graham and Molly Ennis

Sidran Institute Press
Baltimore, Maryland

"The Alchemist" is reprinted with minor changes from Allan Chinen, *In the Ever After Fairytales and the Second Half of Life* (Chiron Publications, 1990) by permission of the author and publisher.

"Inktomi" is adapted from the Sioux tradition as a "retold" tale. Similar renderings have appeared in *Parabola*, vol. 25, no. 2 (2000) and *Zitkala-Sa: American Indian Stories, Legends, and Other Writings* (Penguin Books, 2003).

"The Cave of Truth" is adapted from an anonymous source.

Text and cover design by Lesli Lai Sederquist

Printed in the United States of America

Library of Congress Cataloging-in-Publication Data
Harris, Maxine.
The twenty-four carat Buddha and other fables: stories of self-discovery/by Maxine Harris; with illustrations by Tracey Hedrick Graham and Molly Ennis.
p.cm.
ISBN 1-886968-14-4 (pbk.: alk. paper)
1. Self-realization—Miscellanea. I. Title.
BF637.S4 H355 2003
158.1—dc22
                                2003014739

Dedication

For my father, who read me my first stories, and
For my mother, who always wanted to know what they meant

Contents

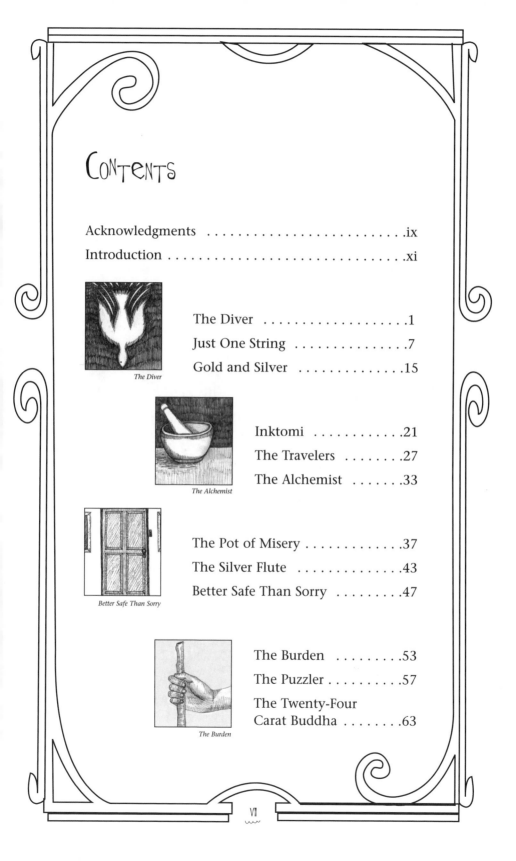

The Diver

The Alchemist

Better Safe Than Sorry

The Burden

Contents

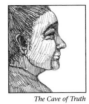
The Cave of Truth

A Language of Your Own

Two Gifts

The Wizard's Message

Acknowledgments

Many people have been instrumental in bringing this project to fruition and I would like to thank them for their support and encouragement. First, this project received technical support from the Center for Mental Health Services/Substance Abuse and Mental Health Services Administration through contract 00M00830101D. Susan Salasin was, as always, generous, creative, and gracious in her personal and professional support.

Esther Giller and Jim Schmidt of the Sidran Institute were enthusiastic and thoughtful in their commitment to make this project happen. Colleagues at Community Connections, Rebecca Wolfson Berley, Caroline Mitchell, Emily Moody, Janna Perry, Kirsten Winters, Caroline Quezada, Zintesia Page, and Laurie Owens read all of the stories with care and generated the discussion questions that form the second part of the appendix. Additionally, Rebecca offered editorial comments on some of the stories and assisted with some of the administrative work necessary for preparing the manuscript.

Janet Harris, Molly Ennis, and Mark Smith also read the stories and offered reactions and editorial comments that have helped to make some of the stories more engaging.

I would especially like to acknowledge my debt to all of the storytellers, named and anonymous, whose work I have read and enjoyed over the years and whose ideas have influenced my own in so many ways. And to the muse of all storytellers, thank you.

Finally, I would like to thank my husband, Mark, whose practical and emotional support of this project and of all my work is the foundation on which I continue to build.

Introduction

 I have always been in love with stories. I can still remember my first stories, read to me by my father as I sat nestled between my two sisters, cozy in my flannel nightgown with the ruffled pink collar, listening to the steam radiator hiss in the background. My father read from the Yellow or Green or Blue Fairy Book, big books with very few pictures and lots of long stories that we borrowed from the library. Some of the stories were funny, silly tales that were told mainly for amusement, but those were not my favorites. I liked the stories with a "message," the stories that seemed written to teach some important moral lesson about the consequences of our behavior. And I especially liked the stories that did not end in the predictable way, the stories that made me consider another way to think about my eight-year-old world.

Stories, even simple tales, engage us at the center of who we are. They are not based on facts or how much we really know about the world. In fact, the details of the stories are often fantastical. The squirrels talk, the princess disappears, and the clocks only measure imaginary time. The same story can be read and appreciated by a child, a teenager, a woman in her thirties, or a man in his sixties since each of us responds to the story from the heart. A good story not only captures our imagination but also engages our emotions. We feel sad, or hopeful, or perplexed; we may turn the page with a smile or with a chill running down our backs. But a good story always makes us feel something. And that is why stories are so powerful and so important.

As each of us tries to make sense of our lives, to solve problems, or to resolve old hurts, we look in many directions for inspiration. We seek out friends, mentors, and experts of every persuasion. But sometimes those sources of comfort and guidance are not enough. We want something that transcends our everyday relationships, something paradoxically personal and impersonal at the same time. And so we look to stories, little dramas in which some truth about life is revealed or challenged.

Just a short time ago, a young woman with whom I work presented me with a gift from her travels in New Mexico. It was a lovely piece of pottery, but more than that, it was a perfectly shaped vessel. A bowl that fit securely in my palms, the kind of shape made to hold dreams and aspirations, a place for transformations to occur. As I sat down to introduce these stories, it occurred to me that I had been just that kind of vessel for the creation of these twenty-four fables. So often I had the feeling that the stories were writing themselves. I would begin with an idea, an observation from an encounter, or a conversation and I would assemble a group of characters. From that point on, a story would begin to unfold. Sometimes I found myself surprised by a heroine's lament or a hero's decision. Often the story ended in a way that I would not have predicted.

When I finished a story, I put it away and forgot it. Sometime later, I found myself reading the story as if I were seeing it for the first time. Some stories made me cry; others left me feeling unsettled; some made me feel hopeful. They each had become their own message, perhaps transformed in the vessel of my imagination, but not belonging to me, simply passed through me on their way to somewhere else.

For the reader's convenience, this collection of stories is organized into two separate parts. In the first part are the stories themselves. They are meant to be read one at a time, slowly savored with plenty of time to be considered. Not all stories will speak to all readers. And that is as it should be. When I went back and considered the stories as a reader and not as the author, I found that I had favorites as well. Some spoke to me with a clarity and a truth that felt very personal; others seemed as if they had been written for someone else. I hope that each reader finds a few stories that help make the world a little clearer, if only for awhile.

For many readers, the stories themselves will be sufficient. Others, I know, will want a little more, and for them I have included an appendix. The first part of the appendix consists of twenty-four commentaries, one for each story. These are the thoughts and ideas that informed my thinking as I sat down to write, and since I am a clinical psychologist with almost thirty years of experience, I could not help but include some of my observations on how a particular story might be useful to someone who was trying to grow or heal from hurt or disappointment. My ideas in these brief discussions may be different from your own as you read the stories. The commentaries should not be viewed as the "true" meaning of the stories. They are simply part of what went into the vessel as I sat down to write.

The second part of the appendix consists of a set of questions for each of the stories. For those who want to use the stories as a vehicle for self-exploration, the questions suggest some potential directions. A reader may choose to contemplate the questions alone, with a counselor, or with a group of friends or colleagues. The questions are not intended as homework, merely as assists in taking the reader further on his or her personal path.

Some stories have a way of becoming part of our emotional vocabulary. We recall them when we need guidance, and they have the power to direct our thinking. We do not even need to recite the whole story. Sometimes merely the title is enough to suggest a lesson we need to remember. I hope this volume of twenty-four fables contains some new stories with the power to become old favorites.

THE DIVER

When he was a very small boy, Kanga would spend hours watching the beautiful white and gray birds that dove from the highest cliffs down to the turquoise sea below in search of fish. With ease and no obvious effort, the birds would return to the cliffs, only to dive again and again, their bodies aimed straight down, piercing the water like the lance of the most powerful warrior.

"If only I were a bird," Kanga thought, "I would spend my days diving and flying through the air. Why is it that boys can only run and hunt and swim, but we cannot soar and dive like the birds?"

Kanga watched the birds awhile longer and then he returned to his chores. He told his mother of his longing to learn to dive, but she merely tousled his hair, gave him a hug and said, "My dreamy-eyed little boy, you have much to learn as a boy and a man of our clan. Leave the diving to the birds and come help me in the garden."

But Kanga would often return to the cliffs and spend hours watching the diving birds. He studied their wings, and the way they tucked their heads into their feathers, and how they caught the currents of the wind, and Kanga made a promise to himself that one day he too would dive from the highest cliffs.

As he got older, Kanga became interested in many things. He hunted with his father and his brothers and he learned the rituals of his clan. He spoke with the elders and came to understand the stories of his people, but he never forgot his desire to soar like the birds. When he reached the age of manhood, Kanga went to his father and told him of his desire to learn the art of diving.

"My son," began his father, "you have learned well the ways of our clan and you have been a loyal son to your mother and me. The men in our village are hunters and fishermen. They live on the land and they take food from the sea. No one in our community has ever soared through the air. It is not our way."

"I intend no disrespect to our people, father, but I have always wanted to dive. You must have guessed that I have secretly studied the birds since I was a small boy. I think I understand their ways. Please help me learn to dive," pleaded Kanga with such sincere desire and such purity of spirit that his father could not refuse his request.

"Very well, my son. I see that your desire comes from the heart, but I cannot teach you what you seek. There is, however, a master who lives on the other side of the island who has trained young men to dive like the birds. I will send you to him and ask him to take you on as a pupil. But you must promise me that after two years, even if you have not learned to dive, you will return home and be satisfied to take your place as a member of our village."

Kanga was so thrilled at his father's generous offer that he wept and threw his arms around his father's neck with gratitude.

"Thank you, father. I will not disappoint you. I will be the best and most devoted student the master has ever seen and I will return to you in two years' time ready to take my place among the other young men of our village." And with those words, Kanga ran to his hut to prepare the few things he would need for his journey to the other side of the island.

When he arrived at the home of the diving master, Kanga was filled with excitement and anticipation. At last he was going to fulfill his dream and learn to dive like the great birds that soared above the cliffs.

"Most revered Master," he began, "I am Kanga from the other side of the island, and I am here to learn how to dive. I will do as you request and I will work harder than all the other pupils, if only you will teach me to dive like the birds. My father has granted me two years' leave from the responsibilities of our clan. So, please tell me what I must do."

"First," intoned the master, "you must slow down. You will never learn to dive if you are in such a hurry. Then you must do everything that I command. And finally, you must never attempt to dive until I say that you are ready. If you agree to my conditions, I will gladly take you on as one of my students."

Kanga was so pleased to be accepted by the master that, in the moment, he paid little attention to the master's conditions. He only wanted to know when he might begin his training.

"Why you have already begun!" exclaimed the master. "The first step in any training is possessing the desire to learn and I can see, my young man, that you have desire in abundance. Now go and find a cot in the lodge with my other students and we will begin your work tomorrow."

For the next several months, Kanga did exactly as the master instructed. He watched the birds every day and made drawings of their wings and of the position of their bodies as they dove from the cliffs. He exercised and ran and swam, turning his body into a well-muscled instrument that would one day be ready to dive. Kanga and the other young men meditated nightly and learned to focus their attention, since the master preached that focus and discipline were as important for the diver as athletic skill. Kanga did all of these things, but never once did he dive from even the lowest of the great cliffs.

One day the master gathered his pupils together and informed them that the time had come for them to learn to dive. Kanga could hardly contain his excitement. At last he would learn the skill that had been his great desire since the time of his boyhood. But before the master began the first diving lesson, he repeated his final command. "Remember that you must not dive from the high cliffs until I say that you are ready. Diving may be easy for the birds, but it is dangerous business for a man. Many have died by attempting to dive before they were ready. I will know when your time has come."

For the next year, the pupils practiced diving from the rocks near the shore and from the low cliffs. Many of them became skilled divers, gliding into the water with the grace of the birds, but none of them was given the signal to dive from the high cliffs. Each time a pupil requested that the master allow him to dive, the master responded with the same, "you are not yet ready." Kanga waited until he was sure he had the necessary skill to dive from the high cliffs and he asked, "Am I ready, Master?" The master looked at him with some disappointment and replied, "Not yet, Kanga, but soon."

Kanga continued to practice and study and meditate and again he asked the master, "Am I ready, Master?" And again the master responded, "Not yet, Kanga, but soon." As time went on, Kanga, like many of the other pupils, began to worry that the master would never give him permission to dive. Some pupils even left the master and went back to their villages, convinced that the master would never believe they were ready to dive from the high cliffs.

More months passed and Kanga was almost at the end of the two years his father had given him to pursue his dream. Kanga simply could not understand why the master withheld his consent. Kanga was clearly the best of the master's pupils. His body was strong and his focus was sharp. He knew the birds' movements so well that sometimes as he was falling asleep he even believed himself to be a bird and not a young man at all. Still he could not figure out why the master would not say that he was ready to dive.

One day, Kanga decided that he could no longer wait for the master's permission. He had waited and obeyed for nearly two years, now his time to return home was fast approaching. He knew that he was ready to dive, even if the master did not. He rose early on the morning he had chosen for his dive and climbed with great determination to the top of the highest cliff. For almost an hour he stood completely still and focused on the water below, then with a forceful thrust, he leapt from the cliff, soaring upward for a brief moment, he swung his legs up over his head, tucked his chin into his chest and pointed his body into the sea. Kanga hit the water with such force that he almost lost consciousness, but when he opened his eyes, he saw that he was swimming with the fish. Kanga had indeed successfully dived like the birds into the waiting waters. When he swam to the shore, Kanga was so overwhelmed with awe at what he had accomplished that he knelt down and gave thanks to the air and the sea for allowing him to return safely to the solid ground.

Kanga could hardly wait to tell the master of his accomplishment. "Master, I could no longer wait for you to tell me that I was ready to dive. I ask your pardon, but I dove from the cliff earlier today."

"Congratulations, my son. I have been waiting and waiting for you to be ready. I was beginning to wonder if you would ever realize that the time had come for you to dive."

Kanga looked at the master with disbelief. "But, but," he stammered, "I thought I was to wait until you told me that I was ready to dive."

"Diving," began the master, "like all of the really important actions in life, requires that you possess absolute confidence in yourself. I can teach you the skills you need to dive, but the belief in yourself is something you must take for yourself. No one can give it to you, even a wise master like me." And with a wink and a smile, the master returned to his other pupils.

Just One String

A long, long time ago, before there were computers or typewriters or even paper and pens to write with, people recorded the events of their lives on elaborate cloths called Life Lines. Every child was given a plain cloth at birth by the clan chieftain and the child's parents made the first marks on the Life Line by stitching on the exact time of the child's arrival on earth and recording any noteworthy events surrounding the birth. From then on, family members would add marks or stitches or designs until the child was old enough to assume the responsibility for recording his or her own story. At the end of a long life, a clan elder might have a Life Line that was decorated with all manner of charms and relics and embroidered with brightly colored string, telling of births and deaths, triumphs and defeats, as well as the everyday struggles of living in a village near the ends of the earth.

Gala was only twelve years old, but she was already very proud of her Life Line. She had learned to stitch and sew from her grandmother, who was an expert seamstress, so even when Gala's Life Line told only of some small event, her stitching was careful and straight and greatly admired by others in the clan. Gala thought often of her Life Line and of all the interesting designs she would add as the years went by.

Shortly before Gala's thirteenth birthday, the villagers heard rumors that a group of barbarians from beyond the hills were attacking and burning villages to the east. The clan leaders met and plotted how they would protect the village if the barbarians turned west and came after the grain and wine and other riches that were stored in vast silos all around town. The men talked of how they would fight and defend their families and the women prepared for how they would douse the fires and keep their children safe.

Everyone waited anxiously, hoping that the marauding tribe would spare the village. But then one day the much-dreaded alarm was sounded; the attack had begun. Gala's mother called to her daughter and told her to hide in the root cellar that had been dug under the house for storing vegetables from the recent harvest. Gala grabbed her Life Line and her sewing box and did as her mother asked. The cellar was small and cramped, but there was enough room for one young girl to hide from the devastation that was about to begin.

Gala crouched in the cellar, clutching her precious cloth and through the tears she began to stitch the story of the attack. She stayed underground for many days, subsisting on the roots her mother had carefully stored to feed the family during the coming winter. She sewed and she listened and she tried not to think of what was going on above her. At first Gala heard shouts and hollers and the sound of swords and clubs beating against one another, but after awhile she heard nothing at all, not even the wind or the rain or the other natural sounds that were a part of everyday life in the village.

After many more days in the cellar, Gala decided that it was time to emerge from the safety of her hiding place and explore what was left of her village and her home. As she lifted the heavy door of the root cellar, she could see at once that her worst fears were realized. The home she had loved and shared with her family was now nothing more than a pile of ashes. Everywhere she looked was terrible devastation. The central assembly hall, the sacred lodge, the complex of school buildings, and the rows of homes, all gone, all nothing more than smoldering embers. And not a person in sight. Gala called out the names of her family and friends, but only the empty silence returned her call. Nowhere she looked was there any indication that the village had ever been inhabited. Gala sank to the ground, clutching her Life Line, and began to sob. The world and the life she had known were completely destroyed.

When she could cry no more tears, Gala opened her swollen eyes and looked down at the cloth she was still clutching in her hands. "Thank the Holy Spirits for my Life Line," she thought. "The barbarians may have taken my family and destroyed my home, but at least I have my story." And with that thought, Gala looked down at the cloth in her lap and began to remember the happy times she had shared with her family.

After several more days of wandering through the remains of her village, Gala decided that she must form a plan. She could not remain in her burnt-out home. The winter was approaching and soon it would be impossible to live there without the support of her family and her village. She decided to pack up her Life Line and her sewing basket and some roots from the cellar and make her way east toward the hills. But where exactly should she go? And then she thought to herself, "Of course, I will go to my godmother, Magda. She is the wisest woman I know and she will surely be able to give me shelter and advise me about what to do. And," she smiled, "it does not hurt that she is the most revered sorceress in all the land." After adding a few more stitches to her cloth, Gala packed her few belongings and headed off while there was still sufficient daylight for traveling.

After several hours of walking across open fields, Gala turned into a dense forest where she planned to spend the night. But as she entered the cover of the tall trees, Gala realized that the forest was thick with sharp brambles. The branches clawed at her face and tore her clothing as she made her way through the underbrush. After much struggling, Gala was almost free of the worst of the jagged bushes when she felt a sharp tug pulling her back. Her precious Life Line had become snagged on a tall and angry-looking bramble. She tried to gently free the cloth, but the bush held fast. Finally, as it was growing dark, Gala gave the cloth a sharp pull to free it from the bush. She heard a shrill tear as part of her precious Life Line ripped away and remained impaled on the highest branch of the spiky bush. Gala let out a cry, but she knew that there was nothing she could do. Part of her cloth was gone. She would have to guard the rest as she made her way to Magda's house and perhaps her godmother would be able to help her repair what had been torn away.

The next day, Gala awoke early from a fitful sleep and after a quick breakfast continued on her way. She was traveling swiftly through the woods when she heard a low and sinister growl. When she turned to see where the sound was coming from, Gala found herself staring into the yellow eyes of a lean gray wolf. Although she was startled, Gala was not really frightened. She had grown up with wolves that prowled the perimeter of her village and they were usually quite content with the potatoes, corn, and yams the villagers left for them to eat. "Okay Mr. Wolf," she began in a quiet voice. "I know you are hungry and are eager for the roots I have in my bag. I will gladly share my food with you." And with that, she reached inside her bag and threw the wolf a big fat yam, but as she opened the bag, her cloth fell out as well. As

the wolf grabbed for the yam, he bit into the edge of the cloth. "No, no!" cried Gala, "spit that out, you are about to chew my Life Line." But the wolf was much too busy eating the tasty yam to heed Gala's cries. She grabbed the edge of the cloth and tried to pull it free, but as she did, the wolf became frightened and turned to run, tearing off a large piece of the cloth as he fled into the woods.

Gala began to sob as she looked down at the tattered remains of her Life Line. The wolf had ripped away a very large piece of the cloth and Gala now held only a small part of what had been her story. "I must keep this cloth safe," she thought. "It is all I have left of my old life. I will tuck it inside my blouse and keep it close to my heart. I cannot lose any more of my cloth before I arrive at Magda's. I must hurry on my way."

Gala traveled for several more days and kept her Life Line secure inside her blouse. She had only one narrow stream to cross and then she would be safely in the garden of her godmother. As she was about the take her final step onto the shore, Gala slipped on a moss-covered rock. As she fell into the water, the swift current began pushing her downstream. Gala struggled to recover her balance, reaching for branches on the shore and waving her arms over her head. As the water rushed over her, Gala could feel her blouse being thrust up over her head. She looked up to see the last remnant of her cloth being carried over the rocks and into the rushing water. Gala stretched her arm and reached with all her strength, grasping at the cloth and struggling to fight the current at the same time. Minutes went by, and when Gala found herself thrown to the shore, far downstream from where she had first entered the water, she looked at her clenched fist. All that remained of her precious Life Line was a single red string.

Gala sobbed and sobbed and fell to the ground. Brokenhearted and exhausted from her journey, she fell into a deep and troubled sleep, not to be awakened until the next morning by the gentle touch of her godmother. "Oh Godmother," she cried at the sight of the old woman. "So many awful things have happened. My village has been destroyed, my family is gone, and I have lost my Life Line, all but this one string." Gala blurted out her story amidst sobs and desperate gasps.

"There, there, my child, I know all that has happened. I have been waiting for you to find me. Come, I will get you some warm clothes and we can talk."

"But what about my string?" blurted Gala. "I have lost everything."

"We will talk of that too," said her godmother as she took Gala by the hand to lead her back to the house by the stream.

Magda hoped that her goddaughter would calm down once she was inside the safety of the cottage, but Gala was inconsolable. The loss of her cloth had brought back all of the grief and sorrow of the last several months. Magda could see that her goddaughter would be unable to rest until something was done about her Life Line.

"Here, my child, give me the single string that remains of your Life Line," the wise woman lovingly demanded.

"But it is all I have," cried Gala as she clutched the red string to her chest.

"I will not harm your string," reassured Magda, "just place it in my hand."

The young girl took all that she had left of her precious Life Line and placed it tentatively in her godmother's warm palm. As the old woman closed her fingers around the single string, she lifted her hand to her lips and began to blow. As her breath grew stronger, Gala could hear a soft whisper emanating from inside her godmother's closed fist. The old woman gave one more substantial puff of air and opened her hand. As she did, the voice of the string grew louder and more certain. The string began to tell the story of Gala's life. It told of her birth and her family, of all her happy times and finally of the attack on her village. The voice of the string told of all the events that Gala had carefully sewn into her Life Line.

"How it that possible?" cried Gala. "How is it that

a single string can tell my whole story?"

"Why, my dear, all you need is just one string, for every part of us contains all that we are."

Gala reached for her string and held it to her heart. Her Life Line had been saved after all.

GOLD AND SILVER

Isadora had been Queen for as long as anyone could remember. There must have been a time when her father had ruled, but those days were long past. When people thought of the royal palace or of the throne of power, they thought only of Isadora. And it seemed to many that she would be Queen forever.

Each year the royal family held a festival to honor the Queen's birthday and people traveled from all over to help her celebrate. People came to enjoy the delicious food prepared by the royal cooks and they came to hear the sweet music performed by the court musicians, but most of all they came to see Isadora's beautiful garden. For in addition to being Queen, Isadora was also the most accomplished gardener in all the land. People everywhere talked about Isadora's remarkable skill in the garden. Not only were her flowers bigger and more fragrant than those grown anywhere else, but she also displayed the most exotic variety of plants that anyone had ever seen. Isadora knew that her garden was quite spectacular and she was very proud.

The years passed and Isadora continued to rule the land with strength and justice and to tend her garden with care. As the end of her life approached, Isadora began to worry about what would happen to her garden after she was gone. Her only daughter had shown little interest in tending the garden. She was more concerned with wearing beautiful gowns and attending lavish parties. Isadora thought and thought about who might have the skill and the desire to tend her garden. And then she remembered her two young nieces. She had not seen the twin girls for many years, but she remembered fondly how eager the girls had been to learn about the garden and to help their royal aunt tend the plants and water the flowers.

The Queen sent word to her brother that she would like to see her nieces again before she died. Her brother, who was very fond of Isadora, arranged for his daughters to travel to the palace to see their aunt. The two girls, who had been named Gold and Silver by their parents, were filled with curiosity about what the Queen might want with them and they eagerly prepared for their journey.

When they arrived at the palace, the twins were taken immediately to the Queen's garden. Isadora watched from her window as the girls began to explore and to examine the many beautiful flowers and plants that graced the garden terraces. After leaving them alone for several hours, Isadora made her appearance.

"My dear Gold and Silver," she began as she reached out her arms to embrace the two girls. "How very glad I am to see you after such a long time. I have been watching you from my window as you have wandered through my garden. I can see by the way you admire my plants that you have the eye and the temperament of gardeners. Come and sit by my side and tell me what you know about tending a garden such as mine."

The girls, who did indeed love gardening, were eager to share what they knew with their aunt and were filled with questions of their own about how some of the flowers had come to be so big and beautiful. "Of course we know how to tend a garden," they chimed almost in unison. We have helped our mother plant the seedlings and weed the flowerbeds since we were just little girls. Now we help fertilize the plants and prune the shrubs in the fall. We have even helped to tend the orchids that grow inside our mother's greenhouse."

As the sisters finished their litany of accomplishments, the Queen leaned back with a smile on her face. "I can see that you two know much about how to care for a garden, and I have invited you here because I want you to care for mine after I am gone. But there is one more thing that I must know before I trust you with the care of my most precious garden."

"Ask us whatever you want," the twins replied with a sense of confidence and anticipation.

The Queen held both of the girls in her gaze for quite awhile and then she asked, "Do you know how to love the garden? Because that is the secret to having the most spectacular garden in all the land."

As the Queen uttered those words, the two sisters looked at one another in amazement. They had expected their aunt to ask something very technical about how to care for a garden. They had not expected her to ask them about whether or not they could "love" the garden.

"Why of course we know how to love a garden. There is nothing we would rather do than spend time in the garden."

"Very well," responded the Queen, for she was growing tired and her time for making a decision about her garden was growing short. She knew that the sisters had answered her question simply and with a pure heart, but without a real understanding of its full measure.

After all, it had taken her a lifetime to find out how to love the garden in her own way.

The Queen took the right hand of each sister and placed them between her own warm hands and spoke to the twins for the last time. "I will entrust the two of you, precious Gold and shining Silver, with the care of my garden. It shall become your very own to care for as long as you live. But remember, when the time comes for you to pass from this life to the next you will have to answer to the Mother of all Nature for your stewardship of this garden as I now must do for my years as the garden's caretaker." And with those words, the Queen closed her eyes and passed away.

The entire kingdom mourned for the Queen, and after a funeral ritual that lasted several days, she was laid to rest under a willow tree in her favorite corner of the garden. Very soon after the royal mourning came to an end, the two sisters moved into the palace to take up their responsibilities as the stewards of the Queen's garden.

"We have been given a great opportunity and an awesome responsibility," said Gold as she turned to her sister. "We must make sure that nothing happens to this garden. We must guard it and protect it, so that at the end of our time we can say that we loved the garden well."

"Of course, you are correct, my wise sister, but we must also find time to lie in the grass and smell the sweet flowers," reminded Silver, who was the more lighthearted of the two.

The years passed and the two sisters faithfully went about their tasks in the garden. They weeded the flowerbeds and pruned the shrubs. They planted new varieties of herbs and fed the flowers with their own special mixture so that the blossoms grew to be even larger and more fragrant than in the Queen's time. And whenever she had extra time, Gold would think about how she could keep the garden safe from harm. "What if there is a terrible storm," she thought. "A very strong wind might be enough to blow down some of the oldest and rarest trees. I will build a strong hedge so that the winds will be kept from the garden."

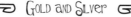

After the hedge was built, Gold began to worry that beetles might invade the garden and damage the plants. Every morning, she would go into the garden and examine all of the plants, removing any beetles that might be hiding under leaves or petals. It seemed that Gold always found some new danger to worry about.

When her sister asked her why she worried so about the garden, Gold replied, "I love the garden and I so want to make sure that it stays safe and beautiful."

Silver loved the garden too, but in her own way. She spent the time after her work was done building a swing to hang from the bough of the willow tree that had given her aunt so much pleasure. Once the swing was complete, Silver enjoyed her free time swinging in the breeze, glancing up at the trees and smelling all the wonderful scents of the garden.

The years passed and the sisters tended the garden and watched it grow and flourish. Many commented that the garden had never looked better, even in the days of Queen Isadora. The sisters enjoyed their role as stewards of the garden and they lived well for many, many years. The time soon approached when the sisters would pass from this life into the next. They spent their last hours walking in the garden and surveying its beauty. They knew that they would have to answer to the Mother of all Nature about how they had cared for the garden and they felt satisfied with a job lovingly and well done.

As they stood before the Mother of all living things, Gold and Silver were awed by the majesty before them. Everywhere they beheld the most magnificent plants and animals they had ever seen. As they gazed in wonder, the Mother of all Nature began, "Gold and Silver, nieces of Isadora and stewards of the palace garden, I welcome you to the next life. I have watched with great interest as you have cared for the royal garden. You have done your job well and the garden has flourished under your care. But you must now each tell me how you have loved the garden."

Gold spoke first, "Heavenly Mother, I have loved the garden beyond measure. It has been my responsibility to keep the garden safe from all harm. I have worried and watched and taken all manner of precautions to ensure that no damage would happen to the plants and flowers. Many nights I have stayed awake, making sure that the garden was protected and secure."

"Well done, Gold. I can see that you have been a fine protector of the garden and all that is in it. You have shown your love by keeping the garden safe." With those words she turned to Silver, "And you, Silver, how have you loved the garden?"

"I have shared with my sister in the daily tending of the garden. But when I have had free time I have tried to enjoy the garden. I have played and laughed and sung in the garden and built a swing for all to enjoy."

"I can see that you too have loved the garden," said the Mother of all Nature. "I am well pleased with both of you and with the love and care that you have shown to the royal garden. You have both devoted your energies to caring for my plants and flowers. A garden needs a protector and it also needs someone to enjoy its many gifts. Together you have cared for the garden completely."

As the sisters walked away from the presence of the Heavenly Mother they both felt pleased, but Silver had an extra smile on her face. She was remembering all the fun she had had.

INKTOMI

In the days of the Old Kingdom, Inktomi was the largest and most magnificent spider in the land. But poor Inktomi was not satisfied being a big hairy spider. He lamented that he was ugly and awkward. "My legs are too long," he wailed, "and my color is too dark." Wherever Inktomi went, he complained bitterly about how ugly he was and about how he longed to be different. All who met him felt that Inktomi was very pitiful indeed.

After awhile, the yearning for change became

so powerful that Inktomi set off on a journey to find the "best thing in the world." As he set out, Inktomi was not exactly sure what he was seeking; he only knew that it must be something different from what he already possessed and that it must be the "best."

After many days of traveling, Inktomi saw a beautiful bird with magnificent blue and purple feathers that hung all the way to the ground. As he looked at the bird, Inktomi was filled with intense longing. Surely this bird was the best thing in the world.

"Oh, how I hate myself," Inktomi wailed. "If only I could be different."

The beautiful bird heard his lament and offered to change Inktomi. He would grant the spider the gift of magnificent and bountiful plumage, plumage that shimmered in the sunlight and would be the envy of all who saw it.

"I will change you," promised the bird, "but you must accept one condition."

"Anything," responded Inktomi, without even asking what the condition was.

"As you will," replied the bird. And with those words, Inktomi was transformed into a creature with long and beautiful plumage.

After several hours of parading around in his new plumage, Inktomi began to notice something odd. His feathers were so heavy that he could barely walk, much less fly.

"What kind of bird am I who cannot fly?"

"That's the condition," intoned the original bird. "I have granted you plumage just like mine, but you must recognize that feathers are heavy and awkward, especially if you are not accustomed to wearing them all day. And of course since you still have the body of a spider, you are not built, as I am, for flight."

"Oh dear," thought Inktomi, "what have I done? I have not been changed into a graceful bird with beautiful feathers, I am just a big hairy spider, dragging a train of feathers behind me." And with that thought, he began to weep.

When he saw Inktomi's distress, the bird took pity on him and asked Inktomi if he wanted to be returned to his original state. "If you want me to remove the feathers," suggested the bird, "I can do so. All you have to do is nod your head and the feathers on your back will disappear at once."

Inktomi shook his head with such force that he almost shook the feathers from his body. When he turned to look behind, he was delighted to see that the feathers were indeed gone. In fact he thought, "my skinny legs don't look so bad after all." But within a short time, the spider once again grew dissatisfied with his appearance and decided to continue his quest for "the best thing in the world."

As he prepared for his journey, Inktomi looked to the sky to pray for success and at that very moment, he saw a finely carved arrow fly through the air. Inktomi saw how swift and straight it flew and said, "to fly like an arrow is surely the best thing in the world." The arrow heard his cry and landed gently at his feet. "I can change you into a creature with the power to fly as straight as an arrow, if that is what you would like, but there is one condition."

"I would give anything to fly like you," pleaded Inktomi, again without asking what the condition might be. Within minutes, he was flying through the air. He flew straight and swift, but when he tried to twist and turn, he was unable to change his course. Inktomi fell to the ground.

"That is the condition," called the arrow, "we can only fly in a straight line."

"Flying in a straight line is very beautiful," lamented Inktomi, "but I will surely starve if I cannot move in circles so that I can create my web. If I can only spin a web of straight lines, all of my prey will escape from my snares quite easily. A spider who cannot trap his food is hardly a spider at all."

"Very well," remarked the arrow, "but you asked to fly with grace and precision and I have granted your wish. If you would prefer being just a plain spider again all you must do is shake your head and you will be returned to your original state."

Once again disappointed with his choice, Inktomi shook his head and was returned to the body of a spider. As he sat in the grass feeling sorry for himself, a young fawn came by. Inktomi looked up and was struck by how beautiful the markings on the fawn's face looked in the sunlight.

"How did you get such beautiful markings?" he asked.

"When we are very young," began the fawn, "our mothers dig a hole in the earth just big enough for us to fit. We curl into the hole and the members of the family cover us with sweet meadow grass. Then our mothers light the grass with fire for just a moment and when we emerge from the hole we are marked exactly as you see me now."

"That's it!" cried Inktomi. "Beautiful markings are surely the 'best thing in all the world.' Beautiful markings will not weigh me down like the feathers of the purple bird and they will not prevent me from hunting like the straight path of the arrow. I will begin at once and change myself just as the fawn has described."

"I can change myself without any assistance," he shouted to the fawn that had begun to nibble on a fresh green lilac bush. Inktomi began to dig his hole. He covered himself with an abundance of sweet grass and lit the fire, and as he did, he declared, "This will be the best thing in the world."

The fire burned for a very long while and when it died down, all that remained was a charred body. Several animals from the forest had seen the flames curling in the air and had come close to see what was going on. "Oh no!" gasped one frightened chipmunk. "It is the body of the great spider Inktomi." "How can you tell it is he?" asked a sparrow. "All I see is a burnt body." "I would recognize Inktomi anywhere by the beautiful markings on his underside. You see, in the forest I hunt for nuts and berries under the trees, and when I look up

I can see the underside of all the creatures. I always thought that Inktomi had the most magnificent markings on his belly. What a shame that some silly fool has burnt him to a crisp."

The Travelers

It was late afternoon when the luxury yacht carrying fifty wealthy European tourists and a staff of equal size sailed into the harbor of the island they called Ile Perdu, the Lost Island. They had traveled for many days to reach the island that few outsiders ever had the privilege of seeing, much less spending several days exploring. The travelers were poised on the deck, cameras in hand, as the crew prepared to drop anchor. On the shore, a small group of native inhabitants stood smiling and waving as the ship drew near. "Welcome to Mikki,"

called one bright-faced girl who rushed to the front of the group, waving and gesturing with both hands.

"What is Mikki?" asked one of the passengers who had heard the girl call out. "Oh, that is the name the native people have given to their island. I think it means 'place of comfort' in their language," replied the ship's captain who was also somewhat of an expert on native customs and beliefs.

As the travelers prepared to disembark for their first real look at Ile Perdu, the captain gave them a brief history of the island. "Because of its remote location only one or two ships a month ever come to the island, so the world you are about to see is as untouched by our civilization as any place you are likely to find. The natives are friendly and welcoming and many of them have learned to speak some English because of the ships that have been coming here. Also, there was a missionary who spent time here many years ago, and he taught a group of the older inhabitants to read and write a little. Some of those skills have been passed down to the current inhabitants. But of course we have not come all this way to visit with a small group of natives. You have come to see some of the most beautiful and awe-inspiring scenery and some of the most unique vegetation and animal life anywhere in the world." And with those words, he instructed his crew to prepare the small rafts that would take the passengers ashore for their first look around.

As the passengers came ashore, the group of natives bid them welcome and then dispersed to go about their afternoon routines. Only the girl with the bright face and dark eyes stayed behind. She offered the travelers sweet fruits that she carried in a basket, hanging from a cord tied around her waist. She chatted animatedly, using words from her native language mixed with English and a word or two of

Spanish that she had learned from the last boat of travelers to sail into the harbor of her island just a few weeks earlier. The girl tagged along as the travelers made their way up a narrow path to the top of a gentle hill. What they saw when they arrived at the top of the hill made everyone stop and just stare. The valley below was the most spectacular combination of pink and purple flowers. The usual green and brown shades of most valleys were almost completely absent. Everywhere there was purple, pink, and more purple. It was as if some wild artist had sprayed pastel paints as part of a lavish prank. Once they caught their breath, the travelers asked questions about how this incredible combination of colors had come to replace the more usual colors of the valleys they were accustomed to seeing back home. The questions were followed almost immediately by the clicking of cameras, a ritual that went on until everyone was satisfied that they had taken the perfect picture. Without a photograph, how would anyone back home believe that they had actually seen a purple valley!

The young girl had seen many tourists gasp and marvel at the sight of her purple valley. She still could not understand what all the fuss was about. She had seen the valley in just this way ever since she first walked to the top of the hill with her mother many seasons ago. She spent hours playing in the valley with her brothers and sisters, made wreaths from the dried flowers she gathered, and sat picking blossoms on afternoons when she just wanted to be alone. She was glad that the travelers liked her valley; she just could not understand what they found so special.

Over the next several days the travelers spent more time exploring the island. They saw the birds with the bright blue feet that splashed in the water like playful children. They watched as the flying squirrels scooped berries from the bushes with a lower jaw that looked like a shovel. And each time they marveled at what they saw and clicked frantically with their expensive cameras. The girl continued to accompany them on their excursions and each morning she met them as they disembarked from their boat with her offering of fresh fruit and flowers. They tried to give her coins in exchange for her gifts, but she had learned long ago that she had no use for the coins or paper money they handed her as they smiled and walked by. Occasionally they gave her some sweet treats or a brightly colored piece of cloth the women called a scarf and these gifts she liked very much indeed.

Each night the travelers returned to their ship for an evening meal prepared by a fine European chef and they talked of all they had seen and of how beautiful the island was and how incredible some of the animals and plants were. And each night the young girl returned to the straw and wood hut she shared with her large family for a meal of fruits, vegetables, and fish that her parents and older brothers and sisters had gathered and caught earlier in the day. The people on the ship went to sleep content, after listening to music and sipping wine and watching the stars from the deck of the yacht. The little girl and her family too watched the stars, told stories, and listened to the sounds of the island and the sea.

All too quickly, the time the travelers had planned to spend on Ile Perdu came to an end. As they walked on the beach for the last time, they watched some of the native children swimming with the sea lions. The young children, whose brown bodies were almost indistinguishable from the sea lion pups, would hold a piece of fish in their mouths and let the pups swim up and grab the fish. The children giggled and swam as the tourists watched and clicked their cameras one last time. The girl with the bright face walked to the edge of the shore and waved as the boat prepared to sail. "Thank you for coming to Mikki," she called and waved some more.

As their ship sailed away, the travelers began to talk among themselves about the wonderful experience they had just had.

"My friends back home just won't believe what we saw. Some of those animals seem straight out of a fairy tale. And weren't the sunsets over the purple fields just spectacular!" exclaimed one passenger. "Everything was truly marvelous," said another. "You can see why they call this the Lost Island." "I agree with everything you've said," pondered a rather buxom woman with jet-black hair, "but I couldn't help feeling sorry for the native people, especially that bright-faced little girl who kept bringing us fruit. Their island may be beautiful, but they know so little of the world. They have never heard classical music, or read a good book, or gone to the theater. They don't even know that Paris and New York and Hong Kong even exist! Their whole world is limited to that one tiny island."

Standing on the shore watching the ship disappear, the little girl was having thoughts of her own. "Those travelers were very nice," she thought. "And my uncle tells me that they are all very rich and have much power, but how sad for them that they had to leave Mikki. They never got to see the turquoise scorpion fish or ride the waves just before sunset or see the hill that spews fire when the night sky is almost black. They will return to their homes and their families, but most of them will never have a chance to come again to my wonderful island. How very, very sad to only have one week in your whole life when you can walk the shores of Mikki."

THE ALCHEMIST

Many centuries ago, when people still felt comfortable admitting that they believed in magic, there lived a young man who was determined to make his fortune by practicing the ancient art of alchemy. Alchemy was part science, part magic, and part spiritual quest, and if the practitioner performed the rituals in exactly the right way, he or she would be able to transform worthless materials such as stone, dirt, or base metal into pure gold.

While the art of alchemy might seem a simple

way to make one's fortune, the opposite was in fact true. For you see, the exact formulas for performing the transformation had been lost during another era. Everyone knew that alchemy was possible, but no one knew the exact prescription for success. There were some ancient texts that purported to show the way, but these were difficult to decipher. In truth, practitioners of the ancient art had to find the precise formula for themselves.

The young man worked day and night trying to find the exact mixture of elements that would allow him and his new bride to become rich beyond their wildest dreams. While he worked on his experiments, he neglected the work of his modest farm and very soon he and his wife had spent her dowry and were living on the brink of financial ruin. When the young woman pleaded with her husband to give up his quest and tend to their livelihood he refused, protesting that if she just gave him a little more time he would succeed where so many others before him had failed.

When they were down to their last few coins, the young woman went to her father and pleaded with him to intervene and make her husband see reason. Her father, who was a very wise man, agreed to talk with the young alchemist.

"My dear son," intoned the old man, "I received the news of your experiments with great joy. You see, I too practiced the art of alchemy when I was a young man, but although I came close, I was never able to perform the final transformation. Let me see what you have done."

The young man, who had expected his father-in-law to rebuke him, was delighted to show the old man his progress.

"You have indeed done good work, my son," said the old man, "but I can see one ingredient which you are missing. You must gather the silver dust that collects on the leaves of the banana plant. If, and only if, you plant and harvest the bananas yourself, the powder turns to magic and will guarantee your success."

"How much of the magic powder do I need?" cried the young

man, almost unable to contain his excitement and eagerness to get started.

"Ah, there's the difficult part. You must collect two pounds of the silver powder."

"Two pounds! But that will take hundreds of plants at least."

"I know the task is hard," said his father-in-law, "but success will surely be yours if you have the will to collect the silver dust."

"I will do it!" cried the young man, and he set out to market with his last coins to buy his first banana plants.

The young man tilled the soil and planted the young seedlings with great care. For weeks, he tended his plants and made sure that they were free of weeds and other pests. After many months of hard work, the plants grew to maturity and bore fruit. The young man harvested the fruit and carefully collected the silver powder. He used the money from his first harvest to buy more land and still more banana plants. He continued this way for many years, tending his plants and collecting the magical silver powder. He and his wife built a house, had three healthy children and still he continued to grow his bananas. After still more time in the fields, he finally managed to collect the prized two pounds of silver powder. With great excitement and anticipation, he ran to the home of his father-in-law.

"Look!" he cried. "I have managed to collect the powder you asked me to gather. Now show me what I must do to turn dirt into gold."

"Patience, my son. You shall have your gold, but first we must ask your wife to join us for this experiment."

When the old man's daughter appeared, he asked her what she had done with all the bananas the couple harvested for so many years.

"Why I took them to market and sold them," she replied.

"And what did you do with the money?"

"Why I saved most of it dear father, just as you told me to do.

Here it is in these three large sacks." And with that she emptied piles of bright gold coins onto the floor.

Her father looked at the coins and smiled. Next to the pile of coins he placed three small piles of dirt, and then he turned to his son-in-law. "See, my son, how your silver powder has turned the dirt of your fields into piles of gold."

At first the son-in-law looked perplexed, then he frowned and tightened his brow in an angry grimace, and then, after a few more minutes, he burst into a loud and deep laughter.

"You, my dear and wise father, and not I are the greatest alchemist of all, for you have managed to turn a young and idle dreamer into a prosperous and hard-working man."

The Pot of Misery

The storms had been very bad two winters ago and many people in the village had lost their homes, or their crops, or some of their farm animals. But no one had lost more than young Elena.

Elena had been helping her mother prepare the evening meal when the first winds began to blow. Her two sisters were playing in the yard and her father and older brother were out in the fields trying to bring the cows into safety. She only caught a momentary glimpse at the large funnel cloud before it swept into her yard and her home and everything she held dear. In an instant everything went black and when Elena woke up several hours later, her whole world had changed. Her home was gone, completely swept away by the force of the storm. Her mother and sisters lay crushed under the weight of a huge tree that had been carried from a neighbor's yard by the powerful winds, and her brother and father were missing, gone without any trace at all.

At first the other villagers marveled at Elena's survival and told her how lucky she was to be alive, but when they allowed themselves to realize the full extent of Elena's loss and the depth of her sorrow, they merely shook their heads and whispered to one another, "Poor Elena, how very, very sad to lose so much, poor girl."

As time went on, the villagers began to recover from their losses; they rebuilt their homes and plowed the fields once again. At harvest time people danced and sang and drank strong cider, just as they had before the big black cloud had descended and destroyed so much of the village. Everyone began to recover and return to normal life, except Elena. She kept to herself and rarely spoke. She lived in a small hut she was able to construct from some scraps of wood and thatch that she gathered and she did odd jobs for the other village women who occasionally needed someone to help with the cooking or sewing or tending of the children. Mostly, she thought of her family and all she had lost and she cried soft, lonely tears.

At first the villagers tried to console Elena, telling her that she was still part of their village family and she need not feel so all alone. But Elena only looked down and whispered a hollow "thank you." When they saw that their kind words had no effect on Elena's sadness, some of the villagers tried to offer helpful suggestions. "Why don't you grow a garden, Elena? You always had such a green thumb." "Elena, you should move to the village on the other side of the lake where your aunt and uncle live." "Elena, I have a nice young man for you to meet. He will surely make you happy again." But to all of these suggestions, Elena merely sighed, looked down and said,

"No thank you."

As more time passed and Elena remained sad and alone, many of the villagers began to worry about her; besides, they did not like seeing someone so miserable all the time. A group of the village leaders met one evening to discuss what they should do to help Elena overcome her sadness.

"We have tried every kindness," insisted one woman. "Elena's sadness is so deep, I'm afraid that it will never go away."

"Nonsense," declared one of the council of elders. "There is always a remedy for despair. We must just think until we arrive at a solution."

"What if we come up with a plan and Elena rejects it as she has all of our other attempts to be helpful?"

"If we come up with the right plan, Elena will not turn us away. She wants to be happy again just as the rest of us do," said an old woman with a kindly face.

"I think I may have a solution," said a tall man with a very long beard who had been silent throughout the entire discussion. "I have heard stories of a wizard who lives in the mountains and spends his days forging metal pots with magical powers. Each pot has the power to contain whatever sorrow is placed inside of it. If we could get one of these pots for Elena, she could place her misery inside and be free of having to face her sadness and pain every day."

"Does such magic really exist?" asked one skeptic.

"It will be too difficult to find the wizard and ask him for one of the pots even if they are as powerful as you say," cautioned another.

"But we must try," said the leader of the group. "Elena's misery is too much to bear and it will surely kill her if we do not do something to help."

With those words, it was agreed that the man with the long beard would go into the mountains and seek out the wizard and his magical pots. Several weeks passed and there was no sign of the man who had gone in search of magic, but then one day, as the sun was about to set, the villagers saw him returning down the side of one of the mountains and in his hands was a large metal pot. The villagers rushed to the edge of the mountain and waited for him to descend the steep slope.

"You have returned, my friend, and I can see from the large pot in your arms that you have been successful. Come and rest and tomorrow we will present the pot to Elena and tell her of the plan to ease her sorrow." And with those words, the village elder welcomed the weary traveler home.

The next morning several of the village leaders went to Elena's hut and presented her with the magic pot. "My dear child," began the village elder, "many of us have been concerned with how sad you have been these many months since the great storm came and took away all whom you loved and who loved you. We have watched you mourn and have tried to ease your suffering, but until now, we have had little success. Today we come with a magical gift forged by the wizard who lives in the mountains. This pot has the power to contain all human suffering and despair. If only you will pour your anguish into the pot, this vessel will hold it for you."

"Oh gentle and wise sir," replied Elena. "How kind of you to try and ease my suffering, but my loss has been so great that I fear no magic will be powerful enough to help me."

"Please try. You have nothing to lose," pleaded the man with the long beard who had gone in search of the metal pot.

"As you wish," agreed Elena, and with that she lifted the lid of the pot and wept two years of pent-up misery into the waiting vessel. When she replaced the lid, Elena noticed something quite remarkable. She felt better. For the first time since her loss, Elena lifted her eyes to the group of villagers surrounding her and smiled.

As the days went on, Elena began to

feel better and better. She gossiped with the other young women her age; she took long walks by the river and picked flowers; and she began to prepare the garden she had not had the energy to sow before. She even heard herself laughing out loud once or twice. But Elena began to grow curious about what had happened to her sorrow. Had the magic pot really taken it away? One evening as she prepared for bed, Elena decided to have a look inside her pot. Her hand trembled as she lifted the lid. Inside the pot she saw what she had feared. All of her sorrow and misery lay swirling inside. Elena quickly replaced the lid and for several days after, she felt sad again. Slowly, however, her sorrow lifted and she began to enjoy her life once more. Many months passed before Elena was again seized by curiosity to see what had happened to her misery. As she peeked inside her pot she once again saw her misery inside. And again she felt sad. But this time Elena was also perplexed. It had now been several months since she placed her sorrow in the pot, yet there it was still swirling inside. It had not disappeared as she had hoped it might.

Elena resolved to find the wizard who had forged the magic pot and see if perhaps she was doing something wrong, something that was preventing her pain from going away forever. She prepared herself for the journey to find the wizard and began hiking into the hills. When, after several days of climbing, she found the wizard, Elena presented her dilemma.

"Oh most powerful wizard, first I must thank you for the gift of the magic pot. It has indeed held my sorrow and I am able to feel happy for the first time since my family was taken from me. But I fear that my misery is still inside the pot. It has not disappeared and if I look inside, I can see my pain again and I feel sad. What am I doing wrong that the pot has not made my anguish disappear forever?"

"Dear, Elena, come and sit by me and be comforted," said the wizard in a most gentle voice. "You have misunderstood the power of the metal pot. The pot has the power to contain your sorrow, so that you are free to live your life again. No power on Earth is strong enough to make sadness and pain disappear forever."

As she heard those words, Elena did indeed feel comforted and she knew what she would do. She went down the side of the mountain to live her life, knowing that the large metal pot would always be there. And she also knew that from time to time she might again be tempted to look inside.

THE SILVER FLUTE

Because the King's only son had died in battle, the King needed a plan for choosing a new ruler who would govern the kingdom with wisdom and courage. The King agonized as he tried to find the right strategy for choosing a successor. The young Prince had been much beloved by his subjects. He was not only known as a fearless warrior but also as a man who could be gentle and kind. And he could charm the people for hours by playing the most wonderful songs on his silver flute. The King remembered his son as he held the beautiful flute in his hands. His son had always carried the flute with him as he traveled from village to village within the kingdom. As he looked at the flute, the King began to devise a plan. He would give his kingdom to the man who could learn to play the flute as his son had.

At first this seemed an easy challenge to the many knights and earls who wanted to be king. What could be so hard about playing a flute? Many tried the Prince's instrument, but the screeching noises they produced only caused the King to wince and the others at court to laugh and snicker. Perhaps it was harder to play this flute than people thought. The rumor began to spread that the flute was enchanted, and only a magician could successfully meet the King's challenge. But a series of magicians and sorcerers were no more successful at playing the flute than the knights and earls had been.

The King began to despair that he would ever find someone to rule his kingdom, when one day a young man appeared at court. The man was handsome and clever and said that he wanted to hear more about the King's challenge. When he heard that all he would have to do to become King was learn to play the flute, he smiled inside and began to think of all the power he would have once the throne was his. But, he thought, "I must approach the old King carefully. There must be some reason why all the others have failed. I will try to win the King's favor before I take the challenge of playing the flute."

The young man approached the aging King respectfully. He asked to see the flute and looked at it with great care. "Your son must have been quite a fine musician to play such a remarkable instrument. I could not think to play such a flute without much practice. If you will give me one year to study and practice, I will gladly play the silver flute and win your kingdom." The old King smiled. At last there was someone who appreciated how special his son had been. At last there was someone who knew how much he still wept for the dead Prince. "Of course I will give you all the time you need," replied the King. "You seem like a fine young man, worthy of my throne." The young man smiled for he knew that his plan to win the King's favor had already begun to work.

Now this young man had very little interest in playing the flute. He wanted to be King, of course, for he liked to hunt and to sit at court and to chase all the young ladies around the palace, but he thought the flute seemed like a silly pastime for a would-be King. He knew he should be learning to play at least one tune on the flute, but as the months went by, he continued to occupy himself with the pursuits that were more to his liking. And of course he continued to flatter and find favor with the King. All he had to do was mention the King's son and the King would sit and reminisce for hours, comforted by his memories of the Prince.

All too quickly, the year of waiting came to an end. The young man had only one month left before he would have to perform for the King. Although he felt confidant that he had won the King's affection, he still felt that it would be wise for him to consult with a master musician and learn to play one of the King's favorite songs on the flute. When he told the musician his desire, the teacher replied, "Of course I can teach you to play, but it will require much work on your part. You will have to come to me every day for the next month for a lesson. On your own, you will have to practice for at least an hour each night, and you will have to pay me twenty pieces of silver for my time and my knowledge."

"What!" cried the young man, "I will not waste so much of my time and money on your silly lessons. There must be an easier way to learn to play the flute."

The young man went on his way and began to think that perhaps the King would give him the throne without his having to play the silver flute at all. He waited until one evening, just a few days before the challenge was to occur, and approached the King with great humility.

"My dear Lord," he began, "I have been practicing the flute for all these many months and although I can play a beautiful song for you, I know it would never equal the music played by your brave son. Let us skip the challenge and find some other test for my becoming King."

"You are a thoughtful lad for honoring the talent of my son, but a King's word is his honor, and I have said that I will give my throne to the man who can play the flute for me. In three days, I will hear your music and the challenge will be complete."

The young man began to feel desperate and with great haste, he made his way to the home of the master musician. "Quickly," he demanded "I need to learn to play the flute immediately. I only have three days before I must play for the King."

The musician looked at the young man with a startled and disbelieving expression. And then he thought for a moment. "I can teach you to play the flute in just three days, but it will cost you 20,000 pieces of silver."

"That is impossible," cried the young man. "Twenty thousand pieces of silver is more wealth than even the King possesses!"

The old man let a small smile cross his lips. "If you want a miracle, my son, you must be prepared to pay for it."

The young man began to raise his fist in anger when he realized he had been defeated. He mounted his horse and rode off to the next village to seek his fortune.

Better Safe Than Sorry

It was mid-afternoon when word first came that there had been a shooting in the busy suburban community. This event seemed unlike the other reports of community violence. There was no obvious reason for the attack. No fight between drunken friends; no tirade on the part of a jealous husband; no robbery gone wrong. This was a random act of violence that left the father of three small boys dead.

When Rosie first heard the news on her way home from work, she just shook her head. "Surely the police will find out who committed this crime," she thought as she took her seat on the crowded bus. "Such a heartless killer could not remain at large for long." That night Rosie listened with interest as the news reporters gave more details of the crime. Local leaders urged the community to remain calm and encouraged people to go about their normal business. "Now just what does that mean," she thought, "normal business. How can there be 'normal business' when there is a killer at large? I will just do a few things to make myself safer."

First, Rosie decided to stop taking the long walks that she enjoyed every evening after work. Ever since she was a small girl, Rosie had loved to walk. In fact, when her mother was alive, it had been one of the few things that they had enjoyed doing together. "It will be sad to stop walking in the evenings," thought Rosie, "but it is always 'better to be safe than sorry.'" She could hear her grandmother's voice inside her head as she said those words to herself. Her grandmother was a cautious woman who often reminded Rosie to play it safe and to take as few chances as possible. Rosie's grandmother had grown up in a poor family where every month the family had to scramble just to pay the rent. "Chances are for rich people," her grandmother would say. "People like us just need to survive." Perhaps her grandmother was right. The walks would need to go, at least until this killer was caught.

As the days passed, the police received hundreds of tips concerning the crime, but none of them led to the apprehension of the killer. Some people thought that they had seen him drive away in a large moving van. Others reported seeing two men on foot; still others recalled seeing someone who looked suspicious in a red sports car. Each night the news reporters discussed the latest developments and each night community leaders urged people to be aware of their surroundings, but to go about their "normal business." Rosie no longer took her walks, but she still felt vulnerable, and when one of the experts on the nightly news referred to the killer as a sniper, Rosie decided to take yet another step to keep herself safe.

Rosie's only knowledge of snipers came from the crime and war movies she watched on television. A sniper could go undetected, hiding in the bushes, or on a rooftop, or in a nearby building. Without the victim having the slightest awareness of what was about to happen, the sniper could strike and kill. It was even possible to be the victim of a sniper while you were sitting in your own home watching the evening news. If she were to be really safe, thought Rosie, that big picture window in her living room would have to be covered.

One of the things Rosie had loved about her house when she first moved in was the light that streamed in through the large window that was the center of her living room. Rosie loved looking out the window, watching the squirrels and birds in her yard, seeing the colors change as the seasons went from summer to fall. But right now, such a wide-open window was just too dangerous. After all, it was as easy for the sniper to look in as it was for Rosie to look out. She would have to find a way to cover that window.

The next day after work, Rosie made a stop at the fabric store on her way home. She would buy some material for a floor-to-ceiling curtain. Now she would feel safe as she sat at home in the evenings, since without her long walks she now spent much more time in her living room. At first Rosie found herself looking at all the light, sheer fabric. "If I must cover my windows," she thought, "at least I will make curtains that are bright and cheerful." But the more she wandered around the crowded store (it seemed that many people were buying material for curtains and shades), the more Rosie realized that sheer curtains would never do. She needed heavy material that kept out all the light if she were to really feel safe from an attacker so devious that he snuck up on people as they went about their everyday lives. Finally Rosie settled on some heavy blue material with a floral print. If she couldn't see the real flowers in her garden, at least she could look at images of flowers.

Once her curtain was complete, Rosie hung it over the big picture window that had given her so much pleasure. She was sad to give up her view and the enjoyment of watching the activity in her yard, but it was just too dangerous right now. And besides, she kept repeating her grandmother's words, "Better safe than sorry."

Over the next several days, there were two more random shootings. The anxiety in the community turned to near panic. People who had felt that their neighborhoods were safe and open now began to question if any place was free from random violence. Rosie continued to listen to the almost hourly police briefings. Without any substantial leads, the police began to caution residents to be on the lookout wherever they went. One no-nonsense lieutenant warned that the sniper might be any-one, even a neighbor or a delivery person, anyone who was free to go about the community without being noticed.

This latest warning left Rosie feeling very fearful. She had assumed that the people she knew were safe from suspicion, but now this lieu-tenant was saying that the sniper might be anyone at all. One of the things that Rosie most enjoyed about the somewhat isolated neigh-borhood where she lived was how friendly the other people were. Many of the residents had lived in this same small community for years. Rosie enjoyed the informal chats she would have with her neighbors as she worked in her garden or walked to the bus stop, and she liked catching glimpses of people as they walked their dogs or rode their bicycles. But this sniper had changed all of that. Now peo-ple hurried to their homes; it was too unsafe to linger on the street corner for idle, friendly chatter. Rosie even noticed that she stopped making eye contact with people. Better not risk looking in the eye of a sniper; better just to get inside her house and close the curtains.

Since Rosie lived alone, these contacts with her neighbors had been one of her main sources of connection once she left work behind. Her neighbors were not her close friends, but being able to say "Hello" and talk for a few minutes made life so much more pleasant. But Rosie was not going to be foolish just for a little conversation. "Remember," she told herself, "better safe than sorry." And besides, her neighbors did not seem much in the mood for sidewalk chatter these days either.

Weeks passed, the police continued to receive information about the sniper, but the killer who had terrorized a community was still at large. The much-awaited "all clear" from the police never came. People speculated about what might have happened to the murderer. Had he moved to another city? Had he committed suicide? Had he just grown tired of terrorizing people? Eventually the news stories about the sniper receded to back-page status and were barely mentioned on the major news broadcasts. Most people went back to "business as usual."

But Rosie was still frightened. What if the killer was waiting for people to let up their guard so that he could strike again? This might be just the time to be more cautious than ever. Besides, Rosie had adjusted to staying home with the curtains closed. When she thought about it, she realized that she really did feel safer that way. "Better safe than sorry," she smiled to herself. And Rosie lived that way for many years.

The Burden

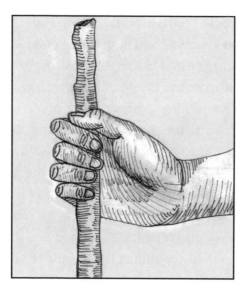

Kimba could not remember when he had first acquired the long stick that he carried with him all the time. He only knew that he could not remember a time without the stick grasped tightly in his left hand. Some in the village thought that the stick had been given to Kimba by a very old woman who passed through the village when Kimba was still a small boy. Others seemed to remember that Kimba brought the stick home from a hunting trip he had gone on with his uncle, and still others believed that Kimba had been born carrying the stick that was his constant companion.

Over the years, Kimba had become remarkably adept at doing all kinds of things without ever putting down his stick. He could hunt and fish and work the fields with the other men in the village. And he was able to eat and bathe and dress himself with only a minimum of awkwardness. Kimba could even dance and parade at the tribal celebrations. Kimba was so good at accommodating to the presence of his stick that many people even forgot that he carried the stick with him all the time.

One day a young woman from another village came to the market where Kimba was selling the corn from his farm. The two talked and laughed and spent the afternoon becoming best friends. After several hours the young woman asked Kimba about his stick.

"Why do you carry that stick with you all the time?"

"I have always had this stick," replied Kimba.

He was puzzled by her question because he could not remember the last time that anyone had asked him about his stick. Everyone just assumed that when they saw Kimba they would see his stick. Someone even joked that he should change his name to Man-With-Stick.

"You have not answered my question," challenged the young woman. "It is not enough to say that you have always had your stick. Think of all the things that you could do without your silly stick. You could run and dance and hunt with a bow and arrow."

"I can do all those things right now, if you please," shouted Kimba, growing angry at the young woman's impertinence.

"Well I know one thing you cannot do if you hold on to that stick. You cannot have me for a friend. I will not spend my time with a man who holds tightly to a stick!" And with that declaration she walked away.

Kimba was hurt and confused and very sad. He liked the young woman a great deal and had even thought that one day he might ask her to be his wife. But most of all Kimba did not understand. No one else had ever questioned his stick. Kimba himself had almost ceased to notice the large stick that he carried everywhere.

Slowly, however, things began to change. Now Kimba was aware of his stick all the time. When he tried to run in the fields, he felt the weight of his stick slowing him down. When he went walking in the woods, he felt the awkwardness of always having to twist and turn so that his stick would not slam into one of the trees. When he danced, he noticed that he could not approach his partner as the other dancers did because his stick was in the way. Now when he gazed at his reflection in the lake, he no longer saw Kimba, the brave young man; he saw only the stick, so huge and imposing that it all but obscured his own reflection.

Kimba became determined that he must get rid of the stick. But how? He had never been without his stick, and on his own, he could not devise a plan for how to be rid of it. Something so important would require the counsel of the wisest person in the land. So Kimba set out to see the Old-Woman-Who-Lives-in-the-Hills and ask her advice. He traveled for many days and nights, winding ever higher into the mountains surrounding his village. Now when he met other creatures along the way, he introduced himself by apologizing for the presence of his stick.

"Hello, squirrel, my name is Kimba. Please excuse my stick, I am searching for a way to be rid of it."

The creatures of the forest just gazed at Kimba as he passed. They had seen many strange things over the years and had learned to look the other way.

After many months of climbing and searching, Kimba finally reached the hut of the wise woman he sought.

"Great Mother," he cried, "please help me with my burden. For as long as I can remember I have carried this stick with me. I have learned to adjust my life so that there is always room for my stick. But I have grown weary of carrying it with me all the time. I now wish to lay my burden down, but I do not have a plan for how to accomplish so big a task."

"You have come to the right place," whispered the old woman in a voice that was as old as time itself. "The solution to your problem is quite simple. See that pile of sticks over there. Just walk over to the pile and lay your stick down."

"What?" cried the young man. "There must be more to it than that. I have come all this way. Please do not play tricks on me old woman. Tell me what I must do."

The woman could see the young man's distress and she repeated her words slowly and with great calm. "You have only to lay your stick down to be free of your burden. The words are quite simple, but the action will take great courage and determination."

The young man walked slowly to the tall pile of sticks. Many looked just like the stick he had been carrying. Others were bigger; a few were quite small. The young man trembled as he approached the pile. But his mind was made up. Slowly, cautiously, he opened the fingers of his hand and let his stick fall to the ground. He turned and faced the old woman.

"Just like that," he said.

"Just like that," she replied.

He nodded to her as he turned and walked down the mountain.

THE PUZZLER

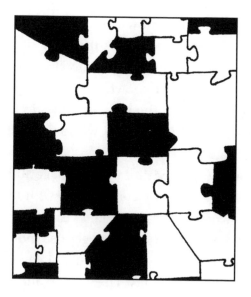

Lena was hot and tired when she finally reached the outskirts of the village. Since she knew no one in the crowded little town, she decided to sit in the central square and rest while she considered what to do next. As Lena sat staring at the people, busily going from one place to the next, a woman carrying a basket of apples approached her.

"Where are you from my dear?" she asked. "I have not seen you in this village before."

As she looked up to answer the woman, Lena began to cry. "Oh how I wish I could answer your question," she replied. "All I know is that my name is Lena, and I have been traveling for several weeks on the road that led me into your village. Other than that," she sighed, "I know nothing more about who I am or where I have been."

The woman with the apples did not know how to respond to Lena. She was puzzled and almost disbelieving as she asked, "How is it possible that you do not know who you are or where you come from? In our village everyone knows the story of his or her family going back many generations. For us, knowledge of family and life history is the most important knowledge you can possess."

Lena had no answer for the woman's question. She could only look away and weep softly. After a few moments the woman took Lena's hand and said, "Even though you have lost your memory of who you are, you are still a visitor in our village and our elders have taught us that every guest is welcome. Come with me and I will take you to my home where you can rest and visit with my family."

Lena was impressed by the woman's gentle kindness, and she rose to her feet and followed the woman home. The woman's house was large and contained many rooms. The woman and her husband and three children lived there, but so did her parents and her two brothers and their families.

When Lena entered the house, an old woman whom everyone called Grandmama, looked up from a large pot of stew she was stirring over an open fire. "Come in child," she called to Lena and her daughter. As the family gathered for the evening meal, Lena once again repeated her lament that all she knew of her identity was that her name was Lena and that she had been traveling for many weeks. The old woman looked at her for several minutes before she spoke. "It is a terrible thing to have no knowledge of who you are. If you feel ready to discover your own story," the old woman offered, "I think I know someone who might be able to help. At the far side of the lake lives a powerful magician. He has the ability to construct a puzzle unique to each individual that tells the story of that person's life."

Lena could hardly believe what she was hearing. Could there really be someone wise enough to finally tell her who she was and where she had come from.

"Of course I must go and see the magician at once."

"Are you sure, my dear child?" asked the old woman, with more than a little caution in her voice. "Some have gone to ask truth of the magician, only to wish they had not."

"I must go," cried Lena. "Not knowing is worse than anything I might discover from the magician's puzzle."

"Very well," said the old woman. "Take this note to him, if you must go, and he will create the puzzle that will answer your questions."

The next morning, Lena set off with Grandmama's note to find the magician on the far side of the lake. After several hours of walking and climbing, Lena approached a small hut on the water's edge. "Is this the home of the magician who has the power to reveal the story of my life?" she called out. After several minutes an old man emerged from the hut. "Who are you?" he demanded, and with his question all of Lena's confidence disappeared. She began to cry. "That is just my problem. I do not know who I am. All I know is that my name is Lena and I have been traveling for ever so long." With that confession, she handed him Grandmama's note and sunk to the grass by his feet.

His voice became gentle, and he offered his hand to Lena. "Rise, my child. It is a terrible curse to be without a sense of who you are. Come into my hut and I will see if I can help you discover your identity and where you came from." As they entered the hut, Lena adjusted her eyes to the dim light. All around her she became aware that puzzle pieces of every size and color were lying on every table and counter in the small hut. "What are all these puzzle pieces?" Lena asked, not sure how all these pieces might help her discover her identity.

"Why these are the pieces of people's lives," laughed the magician. "You did not think that I would just answer your question for you, did you? Oh, no, no, no. All I can do is give you the pieces that tell the

story of your life. It is up to you to put those pieces together."

At first she was disappointed that she would not have her answer right away, but within seconds she turned to the magician and pleaded with him to create her puzzle as quickly as he could. "My, you are an impatient young woman," the magician sighed, for over the years he had been asked to construct puzzles for others who had come with the same enthusiasm and eagerness. "I will make your puzzle in due time, but you must be sure in your own heart that you have the will and the courage to put the pieces together once I have cut them out."

"Of course I have the will," declared Lena. "What could be worse than not knowing who you are?"

"What indeed," replied the magician as he wistfully picked up his tools and began to cut the pieces for Lena's puzzle. For many days he worked quietly while Lena sat in the hut or walked around the lake, waiting anxiously for her puzzle to be done. After fifteen long days, he looked up from his work and declared to Lena, "your puzzle is complete. I have done my part. Now you must put the pieces together and reveal the true story of your past and your rightful identity." With that solemn offering, he put the pieces in a leather sack and handed them to Lena. "May God be with you, my child, and may you find what you seek."

Lena could hardly wait to begin the task of putting the puzzle together at last. She thanked the magician for his kindness and hard work and headed back to the village to find a quiet place where she might assemble the pieces of her puzzle. She found a small room with just a large table and a bed and eagerly began to look at all the beautiful pieces the magician had placed in the leather sack. There were hundreds of pieces of all sizes and shapes. Some were very small while others seemed so large that she imagined they would dominate the puzzle itself. Slowly, methodically, Lena began putting the pieces together. At first she could not make out any definite shapes, but the more she worked, the more images from her past began to emerge. The first part of the puzzle to be completed revealed a large castle set on a hillside. As she put in the last piece of the castle, Lena began to remember a time long forgotten when people called her Princess and her father was a powerful king. The more she saw, the more eager Lena was to complete the puzzle and recapture all of the stories of her past. She worked on her puzzle day and night, stopping only briefly to eat and sleep.

After many weeks of work and anticipation, Lena was ready to add the final pieces. She could hardly wait to see the whole story and know at last who she was and where she had come from. As she placed the last piece, Lena leaned back and stared at her puzzle. A look of horror came over her face. She gasped and cried and flung herself across the puzzle. The room around her began to swirl and spin and before she could get up from her chair, Lena lost consciousness. She lay on top of the puzzle for several hours. When she awoke, Lena swept the puzzle pieces into the leather sack the magician had given her and threw the sack into the fire.

Lena ran from the room in which she had worked so hard to solve her puzzle and found herself walking at a fast pace on the road leading away from the village. She walked and walked for days. After many weeks of traveling, she stopped at a small village for some rest. Since she knew no one in the town, she sat in the central square to decide what to do next. After some time a woman approached her and asked her who she was and where she had come from.

"All I know is that my name is Lena and I have been traveling for several weeks on the road that led me into your village. Other than that, I know nothing of who I am or where I have been."

The Twenty-Four Carat Buddha

The streets of Bangkok are filled with merchants selling all kinds of counterfeit goods. On one corner you can purchase Gucci handbags, on another twenty-four carat diamond and gold Rolex watches, and on the next the latest Nike running shoes. The tourist bureau warns travelers to avoid these "copy cat" items. Most are made locally of poor quality material; some are actually legitimate, albeit stolen, goods; and some merely boast a glued-on logo likely to fall off before the traveler returns home. Despite these warnings and knowledge that they are purchasing counterfeit merchandise, most travelers cannot resist at least one "bargain." After all, where can you buy an Armani jacket for $20, even if it is a fake?

The summer months are among the busiest for tourism in Thailand, and one hot August afternoon found three young Americans among the thousands who crowded the temples and the local spice and silk markets.

"I can't walk another step," groaned Celia.

"Me either," echoed her companion Jean.

"I can't believe the two of you. We are in one of the most exotic cities in the world and you want to rest. Where's your sense of adventure?"

"I think I left it in that last temple we visited."

"Well the two of you can go back to the hotel, but I'm going to explore more of the city." Rachel was determined not to miss one moment of the trip that she and her two friends had spent months planning.

After a bit more chatter, the three friends decided to split up for a few hours. Jean and Celia would go back to the hotel and Rachel would wander on her own. In three hours they would meet for tea at one of the city's floating teahouses.

Rachel had heard about a royal barge that had belonged to the king and she set off to find it. As she wandered the streets, one of the local vendors began to follow her and call out, "Miss, Miss, over here, I have a wonderful watch. Very cheap."

At first Rachel just ignored the man, but as he persisted she became annoyed. She turned and faced the merchant. "I may be a tourist, but I am not stupid. I know those watches are fake."

"Forgive me Madam. You are quite right. These

watches are nothing but cheap imitations."

Rachel was stunned. Here was a merchant admitting that his wares were fakes. She was so intrigued by his acknowledgement that she stopped for a moment to talk. The merchant shared with her his experience selling to the naive tourists and reminisced about the days when his family owned a small antique shop.

"I still have some wonderful treasures from my family's personal collection, if you'd like to take a look."

Intrigued by the prospect of seeing the more personal side of the country, Rachel followed along beside her new acquaintance. The two wandered through a maze of shops, past several purveyors of watches and handbags, until they came to a small storefront.

"Just this way," pointed the merchant. "Please excuse the mess, but I rarely bring visitors here any more."

Rachel was impressed by the small shop that even smelled old and seemed to hold all sorts of treasures. At first she just looked around, taking in as much as she could and anticipating the reaction of her friends when she told them of her adventure.

"I know I shouldn't even show you any of the relics I have here, because some of them are genuine antiques and are therefore difficult to take out of the country, but you seem so interested in what I have here." The merchant then proceeded to remove a small jade Buddha from a dusty case. "This little gem is one of my favorites. I still have the papers certifying it as an authentic antique. Please, have a look."

Rachel took the small object in her hand; it felt so cool and smooth. The little Buddha had a most peaceful smile on his round face. "How wonderful! This is just the sort of souvenir I would love to bring home, but I am sure it is much too expensive."

"You are probably right," said the merchant, and besides, I am not sure that I could part with this piece. You see it was one of my first purchases when I began working with my father."

The two talked awhile longer and then Rachel mustered the courage to make an offer for the jade Buddha. "I understand that the statue is quite rare, but I would be willing to pay $500 for something so unique." Rachel had done the calculations in her mind and figured that if she watched her pennies for the rest of the trip she could just afford the jade statue and still have enough to get back to her apartment in Seattle.

The merchant and the tourist continued to talk and haggle for almost another hour, but in the end Rachel left the shop with the small treasure safely wrapped in her backpack. It was now almost time to meet her friends, and Rachel could not wait to tell them of her adventure and her wonderful purchase.

At the tearoom, the three friends huddled over a small table and a large plate of scones and breads as Rachel began to tell her story. She told of her adventure in great detail, beginning with her curious meeting with the merchant on the street and concluding with her successful purchase of the antique Buddha. Satisfied with her story, Rachel leaned back and waited for her friends to respond. But their response was far from what she anticipated. After glancing at one another, they both looked away, fumbling with their teacups.

"Well?" asked Rachel, growing somewhat uncomfortable.

Celia looked down, her face flushed. She appeared to be suppressing an embarrassed laugh. Jean broke the silence, "Do you realize that you just bought a "genuine" antique Buddha from a man who was selling fake twenty-four carat Rolex watches! It's a wonder he didn't try to tell you it was a Rolex Buddha?"

THE CAVE OF TRUTH

One sunny afternoon several of the young children in the village were playing by themselves.

"Wouldn't it be wonderful if we could be as wise as the elders while we are still young and strong?" asked one restless young boy.

"That would be wonderful!" exclaimed a high-spirited girl. "Then we could make the decisions for the clan and do what we wanted instead of listening to what others have to say. We could play all day and have games instead of chores. Everyone would look to us for answers because we would be called the wise ones."

"But that would not be possible," declared one small boy. "Before you become wise, you must go through the clan initiation and then you must be part of the council and be invited into the chamber of elders."

"Don't be so serious," cried several of the others as they began rolling down the hill and giggling.

The children's chatter about wisdom came to an end as quickly as it had begun, but the idea of attaining knowledge before one's time had found another and more determined audience. While the children were laughing and talking, four young men were setting traps for rabbits in the bushes nearby.

"Those children are certainly silly," remarked one of the young men, "but it would be nice to have the answers to life's many questions before you were so old that it no longer mattered." The young men talked among themselves for a long time, and then they determined to do something about their desire to have the answers to life's mysteries. Together they went to the elder of the clan and asked him, "Wise Father, you have lived many years and seen many things; tell us what lies ahead and what the secrets of the universe are so that we might use that knowledge while we are still young."

"You must have patience if you are to become wise," counseled the elder. "Wisdom comes in time, but first you must live your life."

One of the young men became angry at the elder's response. "You just want to keep the secrets of the universe to yourself. You are afraid that if we gain wisdom, we will take your power away. You are just a selfish and frightened old man."

A faint smile crossed his lips as the clan elder shook his head. "Would that the wisdom of life's many mysteries could be had with just the removal of greed and fear. It is all so much more complicated, but I suppose you will learn that in time." And with those words the elder returned to his tent.

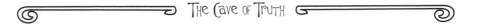

As they walked off, the young men remembered a story that they had often heard growing up. Far in the hills, miles above the village and into the land of the clouds, lived an old woman who was said to possess all of the wisdom of the world inside her cave.

"We must form a search party and venture into the hills so that we might find this old woman and her cave of wisdom and truth," offered the most impatient of the young men.

"It might take many months to find the cave," complained one who was already growing weary with the quest for knowledge. "Perhaps we would be better to just stay here and live our lives as the elders have instructed us."

"Do as you please," said the first young man. "I am going to find a group of young people who do not want to wait years for life's secrets and together we will go into the hills and find this wise old woman. But if you stay behind, do not expect us to share what we learn from the old woman when we find her and learn all that she knows of life."

The impatient young man found a large group of young men and women who hungered for the answers to life's mysteries and were prepared to go into the hills in search of answers.

For many months the group wandered the hills near their village. They met many old women, some of them were even wise and shared their experiences of life with the young people. But they found no cave and no woman who possessed the secrets of the universe. After almost a year of searching, several of the young people decided to return to the village. Perhaps the elders were right after all. One needed to live one's life before wisdom could be found. A few of the party, however, refused to give up. They vowed to continue their quest until they found the elusive old woman.

After many years of traveling, the group stumbled on a cave high in the hills and far from their original village. At last they might have found the woman they were seeking. Inside the cave sat a very old woman who was busy making strange marks on a large tablet. "Oh Mother," they cried, "we have traveled long and far to find you. If

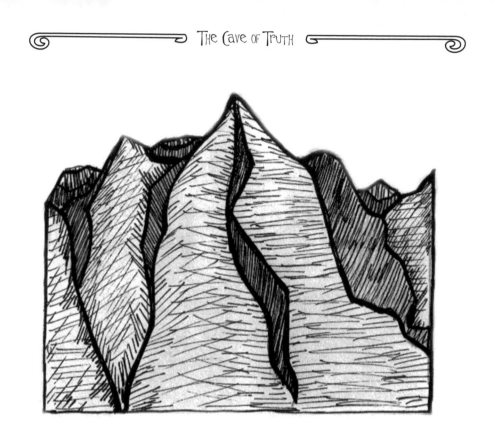

you are the wise-woman-of-the-cave, please let us see the answers to life's questions."

"My children," she replied, "I am indeed the old woman you have been seeking. For years I have sat in my cave and pondered the meaning of my life. I have tried to understand the secrets of the universe. I have sought the truths that will allow me to make sense of my own existence."

The young people could barely control their enthusiasm. The woman talked of "meaning" and "truths," of "secrets" and of "wisdom." She was surely more gifted and wiser than they had even hoped as they searched and climbed all of those years away from the comforts of their peaceful village. She would be able to reveal to them the knowledge they sought. This revered Mother would make their long journey worthwhile.

The old woman listened to their requests for knowledge and truth with tired and patient eyes. She had heard these requests so many times over the years. In fact, she herself had once made the very same request of another old woman in another cave far away and long ago.

"I fear that you will not be pleased with what I have to say and what I have to share with you," she sighed. "But I will show you my tablets nonetheless." And with those words, she lifted the heavy stone tablets on which she had been writing and turned them towards the group.

"What is that!" they cried as if in one voice. "We cannot read those strange scribbles."

"Of course not," replied the old woman. "These marks represent my truth. You must each find your own."

The young seekers heard the old woman's words with a mixture of anger and disbelief. Was this all there was after their years of searching? As they sat together, long into the evening, they talked of their travels and of their dreams. Words of understanding and wisdom fell from their lips. As they listened to the lessons they had learned, they looked at one another. Then they began to laugh. Wisdom was not quite as difficult as they had imagined.

THE CONTEST

Many years ago, when the King was still a young man, his palace was visited by a group of traveling minstrels. Among the troupe was a wise man who delighted in talking philosophy and debating the meaning of life. The King spent many hours with the old man, discussing everything from how to rule his kingdom wisely to strategies for mediating disputes among his many advisors. The King listened eagerly to all the man had to say, and when it was time for him and his fellows to leave the palace, the King thanked him for all he had learned.

"You have been a good student," said the philosopher, "and what you have learned will help you to rule well here on Earth, but if you want to enter the kingdom of heaven when you die, you will need more than philosophical discussions. You will need to answer the one question that has plagued men since the beginning of time 'What is it that makes for a happy life?'"

The King listened to the old man, but he was not sure why that question was any more important than how to win wars or amass riches. The old man saw the puzzlement on the King's face and only smiled. "Perhaps this question does not seem so important now. You have many things to accomplish and a long life ahead of you, but some day, when the years show on your face as they do on mine, you will remember this question." And with those parting words the old philosopher joined his troupe of travelers and went on his way.

Many years passed, and the King governed well and wisely. Many times he remembered his discussions with the old man and used his guidance to make the right decision, but the King forgot completely about the question the old man posed as he was leaving the palace. Until one day.

The King found that as he grew older and approached the end of his life, he no longer cared as much about how to win wars and settle disputes. Instead, he found that as he sat in the palace garden and watched the sunset only one question ran through his mind, 'What makes for a happy life?' And once he began to ask himself that question, posed so many years before by the traveling philosopher, the King found that he could think of nothing else. He thought about this question at night before he fell asleep and in the morning as he woke to the first rays of the sun. It was the first question he asked of every visitor and the last question in his prayers at night.

Now, many in the kingdom wondered why the King was so concerned with what makes for a happy life, since to most of the inhabitants the King's own life seemed the very model of happiness. He had ruled in peace and abundance for many years. He had wed a beautiful princess who not only brought lands as part of her dowry, but who loved him dearly. His sons and daughters were all strong and healthy, and he himself enjoyed every manner of privilege. What more could the King hope to learn of happiness than the life he had lived for the past many years?

Yet the King remained obsessed with his question. He spent hours trying to remember his conversations with the old philosopher to see if perhaps the old man had given him some clue that might answer the question, but the more he thought about what makes for a happy life, the more confused he became and the more despairing that he would ever find an answer.

Seeing how fretful the sovereign had become, one of his advisors offered the following suggestion, "Your Highness, why don't you proclaim a contest across all the land to help you find an answer to your question. A great reward could be promised to the man or woman who successfully answers your question about a happy life."

"What a wonderful idea!" exclaimed the King. "Then I will have all the smartest and most successful subjects in my kingdom and beyond coming to me with their wisdom about happiness. Surely with a competition like that, I am certain to discover the one true answer to what makes for a happy life." The king smiled as he considered all the contestants who would bring him answers to choose from and for the first time in months, he felt himself beginning to relax.

As word spread across the land about the King's challenge, people everywhere began to think about their lives and about what brought them happiness. Many were convinced that they knew the key to a happy life and began planning what they would do with the vast reward the King had promised. Others worked to prepare their presentation to the King, describing in exquisite detail the sources of their own happiness.

On the first day of the new year, all who wished to compete in the King's challenge were invited to come to the palace. The King gathered his most trusted advisors and prepared to listen to the answers brought by his many subjects. After several minutes of prayers and gracious welcoming speeches the chief advisor to the King began, "Who among you is ready to speak first? The King is eager to hear your answers so that he might finally know the secret to a happy life."

With that invitation, one very tall and elegant-looking woman stepped forward. "I am the mother of twelve children," she began. "I cared for them when they were small and taught them well. Their accomplishments have brought me much joy and now my children and grandchildren care for me in my older age. The secret to a happy life is to have a large family with many sons and daughters." As the audience listened to her answer, some nodded in agreement, but others were quick to disagree.

"I, too, have many children," said a man with thick eyeglasses, "but they have not been the source of my happiness. Throughout my life, I have found the greatest pleasure in my books. Every night I end the day by going into my library and reading from one of my treasured books. I have learned so many things and have always felt content with a book in my hands."

"Nonsense!" called a large man dressed in long velvet robes and sporting a brightly colored ring on every finger of his hands. "Books don't bring you happiness. The secret to a happy life is great wealth. Just look at me. I have enough money to buy anything in the world. Throughout my life, I have enjoyed the very best meals, have drunk the finest wines, and have traveled to the most exotic places. My wealth has allowed me to enjoy every possible pleasure."

"Material things cannot bring happiness everlasting," shouted a young man surrounded by a group of friends. "Friendship is the source of true happiness. My comrades and I have been together since childhood. We share each other's sorrows and triumphs and always offer a helping hand. In the evenings, my home is filled with the laughter and conversation of several friends and their families. I am never alone and I know that my friends will always be there to support me. Who could be happier than a man with such fine comrades as these?"

Just as another woman was about to speak, the King rose to his feet. "How will I ever decide the true key to a happy life?" he lamented, holding his head in his hands as he spoke. "Your answers are all so different; one of you proclaims that a large family is the key to happiness; another declares that books and knowledge hold the secret, and still others boast that wealth or friendship are at the heart of happiness. The answers are as different from each other as night is from day; yet you each seem happy and content. How can it be possible that there seem to be as many different answers as there are people in this room?"

And just as he uttered those words, the King knew the answer to his question. He then ordered that the royal treasurer divide the reward equally among all of his subjects.

The Gift of Choices

A long, long time ago, every village in the land was protected by its very own genie. The job of the genie was to watch over the people, but also to bestow a gift onto each newborn child. For awhile, the genies vied with one another to see who among them could devise the most creative and spectacular gift, but after awhile most of the genies grew bored with gift giving and resorted to giving each newborn three wishes, to be used at any time during the individual's life.

But clever Lorna was not like the other genies. She wanted her gift to be something special, but also something that would challenge the villagers to think about their options in a different way. Knowing how difficult it was for humans to make decisions, Lorna decided to grant the villagers under her care three perfect choices. This meant that when a villager was trying to make an important decision, he or she could use one of the perfect choices and thus guarantee that the decision would have the optimum outcome.

The villagers were pleased that Lorna wanted to give them a unique gift, but most of them did not really understand what they had been given. Most of them, you see, thought that choices were no different from wishes, and they treated their new gift much as they would have treated the old promise of three wishes. Lorna had hoped that the villagers would come to see that decisions should be treated with great respect, because sometimes the course of an entire life can rest on even a very small decision.

Only one young girl, among all the villagers, seemed to comprehend the magnitude of the gift she had been given by the clever genie. The girl, who was called Wide Eyes by her friends, would often stare into the open space with great big wide eyes that seemed to perceive a future others could not see.

Wide Eyes was excited by her gift and was determined to use her three perfect choices wisely. She would not waste her choices on silly things like which dress she should wear to the village gathering or what she should prepare for her bridal supper. She would reserve her choices for really big decisions. But that's where things began to get confusing, for how was one to tell what was a really big decision. She remembered her friend who was called Little Feet who had used one of her perfect choices to select a dress for the village gathering. She chose a dress that was so beautiful that Little Feet attracted the attention of the chief's only son and soon was chosen to

become his wife. Perhaps choosing a dress was a big decision after all.

"No, No," she thought, "how silly of me. It is just a coincidence that she was selected to marry the chief's son. Choosing a dress cannot possibly be worthy of using one of the perfect choices."

As she grew older, Wide Eyes spent many long hours thinking of how she would use her choices. She was not quite sure which decisions were really important, but she felt sure that she would know an important decision when she encountered one.

When she turned eighteen, Wide Eyes decided to leave her village and travel to the village of her mother's older sister, who was known to be a wise woman. Wide Eyes wanted to consult her aunt about how she might use her choices. As she left the woods surrounding her village, she came to a fork in the road that she had never seen before. She wondered out loud, "Should I take the road to the left or the right?"

Perhaps this was a decision that was big enough to use one of her perfect choices. "No," she thought, "This is just a little decision. What difference can it possibly make which road I choose?"

So she picked up her silk purse in which she kept her perfect choices, and she walked up the path to the right. As she climbed the steep path, the weather grew more and more ominous. A strong wind began to blow, making it difficult for Wide Eyes to keep her balance. She was about to sit down and think about what to do when she heard a voice calling her from behind a tree.

"Come with me and I will show you a cave where you will be safe from the wind," said the young man as he emerged from behind the tree.

"Oh dear," thought Wide Eyes. "What shall I do? This man is a stranger who might wish me harm, but I do need help in climbing this path. Perhaps I should use one of my perfect choices. No, no, this is a little decision. I will go with the young man and save my choices for something really important." So off she went.

The young man was quite kind and charming. Wide Eyes went with him to the cave and eventually to his village. She stayed with him and his family for many months and the two fell in love. When the young man asked her to marry him, Wide Eyes once again wondered if she should use one of her perfect choices to make what surely seemed to be an important decision. But by this time, Wide Eyes had become so attached to saving her choices and so convinced that things just seemed to work out, that she told the young man she would marry him if that was what he really wanted.

Many years passed. Wide Eyes stayed in the village of her husband, gave birth to six children, lost two of them to illness, learned to weave beautiful blankets, took a young warrior as her lover, quarreled with her husband's sister, and watched as her hair turned gray with the passing years, but never found a decision big enough to warrant using one of her perfect choices.

When she was a very old woman, Wide Eyes had occasion to meet an old man who had been a boy in the village of her family when she herself was a young girl.

"Come sit with me," she called to the weary villager, "and tell me of my family."

"So much has happened since you left that I hardly know where to start. Shortly after you left to visit your aunt, a terrible storm came and flooded all land on the left side of the fork in the road. Many people were killed. In order to rebuild our village we formed an alliance with another chieftain. Your father was asked to pledge his oldest daughter to the chieftain's son, but since you were not to be found, your sister married the young man. He was quite a tyrant, but when he died in battle years later, your sister became our ruler and is now much revered."

"Stop! Stop!" cried Wide Eyes. "I do not want to hear any more. It's too confusing to imagine a different life from the one I have had. Perhaps those things would have happened to me if I had used my perfect choices."

"Ah yes," mused the old man, "the perfect choices. How did you use yours after all?"

"Why, I haven't used them," said Wide Eyes. "I never found any-thing important enough to warrant using the gift of the genie. They are still here in my silk purse."

But when she opened the bag to show her old friend, the two saw nothing inside the faded bag but dust.

A Language of Your Own

The Land Beyond the Hills was a very remarkable place. Everyone there was born speaking his very own language, and yet what made the community so unique was that every villager—man, woman, and child—had the ability to understand everyone else. This skill was so unusual that linguists came from all over the world to study the people who lived in the Land Beyond the

Hills. Professors from all the leading universities came with theories about how such a remarkable skill might have evolved, but no one knew for sure how this unique talent had come to be.

One day, a young man with ambitions for political power made a suggestion to the assembled leaders of the community. "We have a nice life here in the Land Beyond the Hills," he began with a solicitous nod to the assembled representatives. "But we have no discourse with the outside world. Because we speak so many different languages, it is impossible for people living in other lands to do business with us. We need a single language for all of our people."

"No, never!" cried one agitated older man. "That is not our way. We have always each had our own language. It has never been different."

"Well perhaps," said another, "we could try to use one single language and see if we like things better that way."

"Very interesting," pondered a well-dressed gentleman with a feather in his hat. "Think of the possibilities for trade and profit."

The discussion went on for many hours as the assembled representatives debated the pros and cons of having just one language. Some said that the discussion went on for longer than it needed to because each speaker wanted the chance to say his or her mind even if someone else had already made the very same point. After all, the only time a villager heard his own language spoken was when he spoke it himself.

Finally, one speaker offered a suggestion, "Why don't we see if we can agree on a common language. I propose that we spend the next thirty days trying to find the perfect language to represent all the people of our land. Those who think that their language is the best can try to convince others to speak as they do and those who like the sound of another's language can try and see if they can learn a new way of communicating. At the end of thirty days we will meet again and see if we are any closer to selecting a common language."

Some members of the group started to object to the speaker's proposal, but most of the representatives were so exhausted and so eager to get home to their beds that the group agreed to try to find a language that might please everyone in the land. Of course no one quite knew how he or she might go about doing that, but they agreed to the plan nonetheless.

After a few days' rest, some of the more ambitious members of the community began to think of how they might succeed in getting their language adopted as the official language of the land. "I will pretend that I can understand no language but my own," thought one rather pompous gentleman who ran the largest store in town. "Then anyone who wants to speak with me and buy my goods will have to learn my language." He smiled to himself as he thought of how important he would be when his language became the language of the whole land.

Another man who was quite wealthy decided to use his wealth to influence people to adopt his language instead of their own. He went to the center of town and began calling out, "Fifty gold pieces, fifty gold pieces, I will give fifty new gold pieces to any citizen of our land who gives up his own language and speaks as I do." Before long, there was a large crowd gathered around the speaker and several people were attempting to imitate his speech so that they might be rewarded with the shiny coins.

Two young lovers who had vowed to share everything with one another were practicing each other's languages and a boy who did not like the sound of his own speech was trying to imitate the language of one of the town's most learned men. All over the land people were busy either trying to convince their neighbors to speak as they did or trying to imitate the speech of others. Some people who were afraid that their unique languages would be taken away from them decided that the best strategy was to speak to no one and to keep their language completely to themselves. Of course that meant that they were all alone without anyone to talk to at all. For the entire thirty days, no work got done in all the land, no children went to school, and no business was conducted. Everyone was consumed with the task of choosing a common language.

At the end of the thirty days, the town elders and representatives assembled to see what success they had had. Since everyone in the land was curious about the outcome of their deliberations, a large crowd of citizens followed them into the meeting hall. The ambitious young man who had suggested a common language in the first place began to speak, "My fellow citizens, we are here to discuss our progress in selecting a common language." He paused for a moment and looked out over the assembled crowd, expecting to see the usual agreement of nodding heads and eager smiles, but instead he saw only blank faces. "We are here to discuss our progress in selecting a common language," he repeated, only this time a little louder, thinking that perhaps his fellow citizens had not heard him the first time, but again he saw only blank faces, with a few frowns and furrowed brows.

"How strange," he thought, "this is not like my countrymen at all." At just that moment an angry-looking fellow rose to his feet and shouted, "Make sense man or sit down. We cannot understand a word you are saying. You are talking nothing but gibberish." But the ambitious young man could not understand a word the angry speaker was saying, in fact, no one could. The crowd broke into a frenzy of chatter as everyone turned to his or her neighbor and tried to communicate, but no one could understand what anyone was saying. In their attempt to find a single language for everyone, the citizens of the Land Beyond the Hills had completely lost the ability to understand one another.

In the days and weeks following, townspeople tried desperately to communicate with one another. In the cafes, on the streets, and in the shops, people could be seen huddled together, trying to listen extra carefully to one another and trying to form strange words that might make sense to their partners. But all of these strategies failed. No one in the Land Beyond the Hills could understand a single word spoken by anyone else and no one had found a way to make himself understood by even his closest friends and family. After awhile, most people just gave up and stopped trying to communicate at all. Some people wondered how they had gotten into such a mess, but no one had a solution for how to make things better.

Several years passed, and the Land Beyond the Hills became a very quiet place. People hardly spoke at all since there was little point in trying to communicate. When people wanted something in a shop or a café, they would simply point or nod their heads, but no one said a word.

One day, a young girl, who had been only a small child when all the chaos about a common language had stirred up, was walking alone in the fields when she heard a very soft voice. Since she had never spoken to anyone before, she was at first startled by the strange sounds that seemed to be coming from some place deep inside her. "Speak!" commanded the voice. "How silly," thought the young girl. "There is no point in speaking because no one can ever understand what I say." "Speak!" ordered the voice once again. This time the girl listened more closely to her voice. It seemed so adamant that she wondered if the voice had some secret knowledge. "But what shall I say?" asked the young girl. "No one in this land has spoken for a very long time. What can I, a young girl, possibly have to say?" "Speak from your heart," said the voice as it trailed off into silence.

The young girl waited for more communication from her voice, but there was none. As she walked home, she thought and thought about the strange message she had received from the voice inside her.

Soon after, the young girl was visiting with her grandmother who had baked some very special cookies for her visit. "Thank you for the wonderful cookies," said the girl without stopping to think about the fact that she was speaking. "I love you very much."

All of a sudden, her grandmother looked up from her baking, for she could not believe her ears. She had just heard her lovely grand-daughter say "I love you." Very tentatively the grandmother formed the words, "I love you too, dear child," and she could see instantly from her granddaughter's expression that the young girl had understood her words. They began to chatter and laugh and talk some more. They had much to say to one another for they had never spoken. And from that time on, whenever someone from the Land Beyond the Hills spoke from the heart, they discovered that other people understood exactly what they were saying, no matter what language they spoke.

THE MOST EVIL MAN IN TOWN

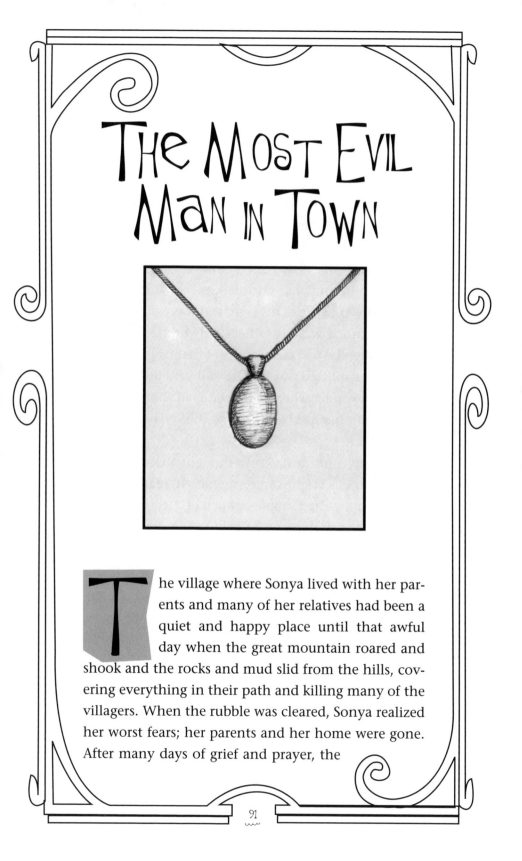

T he village where Sonya lived with her parents and many of her relatives had been a quiet and happy place until that awful day when the great mountain roared and shook and the rocks and mud slid from the hills, covering everything in their path and killing many of the villagers. When the rubble was cleared, Sonya realized her worst fears; her parents and her home were gone. After many days of grief and prayer, the villagers who had survived the disaster met to decide what to do about the terrible devastation and how to care for the many children, like Sonya, who were now orphans. After much discussion and with great feelings of sorrow, the villagers decided that any child who had relatives living in safety, away from the site of the avalanche, should be sent to those relatives. That was how it was agreed that Sonya should go and live with her uncle.

As she rode on the back of the wagon that was to take her to her new home, Sonya realized that she knew very little about the man who was about to become her guardian, except that he lived by the sea, had no children or wife of his own, and was a very powerful man. Even though this uncle was her father's only brother, Sonya had seen him just once, when he had come to visit after her grandmother died. All that Sonya remembered was that he said very little and other people seemed to grow quiet whenever he entered the room. Perhaps he was shy like her mother had been. Sonya would have to take her time to get to know him.

As the long trip continued, Sonya thought about her parents. She could see her mother's bright smile and hear her father singing as he tended the garden that had supplied much of their food. Now, all she had left of those happy times was a gold locket she wore around her neck and a piece of silver her father had given her on her last birthday. Sonya thought about her two treasures and began to cry. She had so little left of the life she had enjoyed.

When she arrived in the village by the sea that was to be her new home, Sonya began to ask the people she met where she might find her uncle. Each time she mentioned his name, she met the same reaction. People looked down and began to quicken their steps away from her. "Oh dear!" she thought to herself. "Perhaps something terrible has happened to my uncle and now I will have no one at all."

At last she wandered into the town church and saw the priest getting ready for the evening service. "Holy Father, please help me. I am one of the orphans from the avalanche and I have been sent here to live with my uncle, but every time I mention his name, people turn from me and hurry away. Please help me find my uncle." "Of course, I will help you my child, just tell me who your uncle is," said the priest in a calm voice. But when Sonya mentioned her uncle's name, she saw the priest's mouth fall open. "You cannot possibly want to see him!" exclaimed the priest. "He is the most evil man in town." The priest's words hit her with the force of the mudslides that had destroyed her village. Her uncle was her only living relative. How could this possibly be true? "Just tell me where he lives," she muttered in a choked voice. "I have no choice but to go to him."

Although he was reluctant to send a young girl to live with a man he knew to be ruthless, the priest gave Sonya the directions she requested, and with a bowed head she left the church and headed to the large house overlooking the sea and the beginning of her new life.

And while her uncle did not greet her with a warm welcome when she rang the bell outside his door, he did not turn her away either. Instead he listened to her story of loss and sadness and he told her she could stay with him in a small room at the back of his very large house if she kept to herself and did as he requested. Sonya was so relieved that her uncle did not turn her away or behave terribly that she accepted his conditions and went exhausted to her little room. But before she had even a minute to put her head on the pillow, her uncle was standing outside her door shouting. "Who said you could sleep?" he bellowed. "I can see that you're a lazy one just like my brother. If you want to eat, you must work. Come out of that room and help the cook prepare dinner." Sonya's heart began to race as her uncle screamed. Her father had been a gentle man and Sonya was not accustomed to yelling. But perhaps what scared her even more than the loud shouting was the horrible look in her uncle's eye. There was no kindness there, only a coldness that made her shake as she hurried to the kitchen, too frightened to remember how exhausted she had been just a few minutes before.

Sonya did her best to do as she was told and to stay out of her uncle's way, but he still found reasons to scream and threaten her. "If you do not behave as I wish, I will have to beat you like the dog that you are," he would thunder. Eventually, the threats gave way to actual beatings and whippings. Sonya could just not understand why her uncle behaved the way he did. Perhaps she was doing something wrong. Perhaps he really was evil like the priest had said. Or perhaps, she thought, this was the way that powerful people got what they wanted.

One day Sonya's uncle saw her looking at the locket and the silver coin she had brought with her from her village. "Where did you get those treasures? You are not only lazy," he cried, "but you are a thief as well. Give me those before I give you a beating you will not forget." "But these are mine," Sonya insisted. "I brought these with me from home. They were gifts from my parents." "How dare you defy me," her uncle shouted as he snatched the gold and silver from her hands and stuffed the small treasures into his pocket.

Sonya's grief at the loss of her only connection to her old life was almost unbearable. It felt as if something deep inside her had snapped. But Sonya continued to live with her uncle. She did as she was told, suffered the occasional beating, endured the almost daily harangues, and told herself that her time would come. One day she would get even with her uncle and then she would be free of his evil ways.

Years passed and Sonya grew into a young woman. As her uncle grew older and less powerful, he came to rely more and more on his competent niece to help him run his home and business. Sonya was put in charge of the house servants and could sometimes be heard all the way down in the street below the big house screaming orders to the cook or the maid. One day when Sonya was bringing her uncle his lunch, she heard a low groan as she entered his room. "Help me, help me," he moaned. "I need medicine. I need a doctor. I think I am dying. Don't just stand there, you lazy wench, do something." Sonya looked at her uncle, but there was no kindness in her eye, only a frightening coldness. She turned and left his room, locking the door behind her. The maid came up behind Sonya and asked if there was anything she could do. Sonya glared at her. "Do your job, stupid woman, or I will give you a whipping you won't soon forget."

More years passed, and Sonya continued to live in the big house overlooking the sea. After her uncle's death, Sonya became mistress of the house and became even more powerful than her uncle had been. He had taught her well how to run a business and a home. But she never married and she almost never thought of her parents, or her village, or the life that had been destroyed by the terrible avalanche.

One day a man from the old village appeared in town. "I am looking for a young girl," he asked the first person he saw on the street. "She would be a woman in her mid-life by now. She and I lived in the same village many years ago. A huge avalanche destroyed our homes and she came here to live with her uncle. Do you know where she might be? Her name is Sonya." As the townsperson heard the name, he cringed. "You cannot possibly want to see her," he warned. "She is the most evil woman in town."

The Gambler's Lesson

For years, the three brothers had heard stories about the remarkable accomplishments of the man known only as the Gambler. To be known as the Gambler was quite an honor in the lands that stretched from the tall mountains all the way to the sea, for gambling was not merely a pastime enjoyed by nearly all the men, it was also considered by many to be the true test of a man's worth.

One day, after they had performed their chores in the fields and were preparing for the evening meal, the brothers began lamenting their lack of success at the gaming tables. "We have watched our father and our uncles and cousins play cards and roll dice since we were young boys and still we seem to have no skill when it comes to gambling. Surely we must be doing something wrong," began the oldest brother. "Tomorrow evening is Saturday night and all of our friends will be going into town to play at the big gaming houses. But we might as well stay home. People only laugh when they see us because everyone knows that we are sure to lose."

"Perhaps gambling is just a matter of luck and there is no skill involved at all," suggested the middle brother, who was less interested in card playing than his two brothers. "If that is the case, we just may not have the luck of the gambler. We are better off staying home and tending our fields."

"Don't give up so easily," insisted the youngest and most impetuous of the brothers. "There has to be a way to improve our skill and our odds of winning. I am not prepared to be known throughout the land as one of the three most unlucky brothers."

Then the oldest brother remembered all the stories they had heard about the man known as the Gambler. "I have an idea," he shouted to his brothers enthusiastically. "We must go to the Gambler and ask him to take us on as pupils. Surely if we tell him how unsuccessful we have been, he will take pity on us and agree to teach us what he knows."

"You are being silly," replied the middle brother, who was growing frustrated with this conversation and just wanted to sit down and have his dinner. "The Gambler must surely have better things to do with his time than try to teach three brothers who obviously have no talent for card playing."

"Of course he will take us on as students," declared the youngest, already thinking two steps ahead of his brothers. "A true gambler cannot resist a challenge, and what greater challenge is there than to turn three losing gamblers into winners! Yes, he will accept us as pupils; I am sure of it."

After a bit more discussion the brothers agreed to get a good night's sleep and in the morning set out across the mountains in search of the Gambler. They would tell him of their woes, but they would also offer him a bag of gold coins if he could teach them how to be true gamblers.

After a day of riding toward the low hills, the brothers stopped in a bustling town and went straight to the gambling house. "Has any-one seen the Gambler?" they called out to the crowd of players who were much more interested in the games that were going on than in answering the questions of strangers.

"Either sit down and play or go away," called one card player who was obviously annoyed with the interruption.

The brothers realized that they would have to play at least a few rounds at the gaming tables before anyone would take the time to lis-ten to their request. They joined a small table of card players and after losing several of the coins from their sack, the brothers once again asked the whereabouts of the Gambler. "He was here a few days ago, but he has moved on to the next town. You can probably catch up with him if you ride quickly to the east," said the only player who was willing to take his eyes off the game. The brothers thanked the player for his information and gathered up their sack of gold and swiftly mounted their horses. But when they arrived in the next town, they again met with disappointment. The Gambler had moved on, they were told, and they could find him if they just rode quickly to the east. And once again, they mounted their horses and rode, but with no better luck than before.

The brothers rode for months, going from town to town and from gaming house to gaming house, always just one step behind the Gambler. Finally, they found themselves back at the first town and sitting once again at a card table with a small group of players when they looked across the table and saw the man who had first told them to ride east. "Excuse me, sir," began the oldest brother, "but we are the same brothers who came seeking the Gambler many months ago. We did as you said and rode east, but we have had no luck in finding the Gambler. We always seem to miss him by just a few days. Please tell us if you have seen him since we were last here."

The player looked up from his cards and looked at each of the brothers. He could see their frustration as well as their resolve. He sat quietly for a few moments and then he answered. "I was hoping you would return. I am the Gambler you seek. I had heard that three brothers were in search of lessons in the fine art of gambling, so when you came looking for me, I assumed you were the brothers. I decided right then that I would give you your first lesson. Gambling requires patience. At the end of the day the true gamblers are the ones who are left at the table. Those without determination get up and leave the game long before the last card is played. You have shown that you have the perseverance necessary. If you are still interested, I will take you on as students and teach you what I know."

The brothers were so astonished that they could hardly speak. They did not know if they should be angry for having been duped or overjoyed at having found the Gambler who was indeed willing to teach them what he knew. In the end they decided to accept the Gambler's offer and begin their apprenticeship. "But we have no money to pay you," said the youngest brother. "We have lost all of our money at the gaming tables."

"You have already paid me," said the Gambler with a smile. "I have won your gold and more. You see, I followed you from town to town and each time you sat down to play, I won a little more of the money you brought as my payment. I have already been paid in full. We can begin your lessons in the morning."

The brothers did not know what to make of this strange man

they called the Gambler. He did indeed seem to win most of the time and he had the respect of everyone, but he confused the brothers with his unusual ways and his cryptic comments. Had he cheated them or just outsmarted them or was he really the best Gambler the land had ever known? It was all too confusing to figure out, but since they had come all this way, they decided to remain as his pupils and see what they might learn.

For the next several months, the brothers were always at the Gambler's side. They watched him when he won and when he lost and they listened to his comments on the fine art of gambling. Occasionally he would let one of the brothers play a hand or roll the dice, but most of the time, the brothers just watched and listened. Finally, the Gambler turned to the brothers and remarked, "You have been by my side these many months and I have tried to teach you all that I know. You are ready for your final lesson." And with those words, the Gambler dealt a hand of cards to each of the brothers and to himself. "You are each to play the cards I have dealt you, as best you can."

As he looked at his cards the eldest brother began to tremble with rage. "These cards are impossible to play," he shouted. "This is the worst hand I can imagine. I have studied with you for many months. I have stayed away from my family and ignored my farmlands. And now you reward my effort by dealing me a hand of losing cards." With those words, the eldest brother pounded his fists on the table and fumed.

Next the middle brother picked up his cards. His mouth fell open and he too began to wail. "I am sure my cards are even worse than those of my brother. This hand is not even worth playing. My cards are so bad I am sure to lose. I knew we should never have come on this useless journey. We should return to our farm and forget about gambling." And with those words, the middle brother slumped down in his chair and looked forlorn.

Finally, the youngest brother picked up his cards. "You have cheated me!" he shouted, glaring at the Gambler. "It is impossible to get such bad cards just by chance. You have obviously fixed the deck so that you would win and we would lose. This game is not fair," he whined, fixing his face in the most disagreeable pout.

Finally, it was the Gambler's turn to look at his cards. He surveyed the hand he had been dealt and sat back and smiled. The brothers, who had already assumed that they would lose, threw down their cards and accepted defeat. As they prepared to leave the gaming hall the Gambler called out, "Don't you want to see the cards that beat you?" And with those words, the Gambler laid his hand on the table.

The brothers could barely believe their eyes when they realized that the gambler had won with the exact same cards that each of them had thrown away. Before any of them could speak, the Gambler began his parting lesson. "Your eyes do not deceive you, my young friends, we were all dealt the same cards. The art of gambling is not about getting great cards all the time. The art lies in how you play your cards no matter what they are. Great cards don't make great gamblers; great gamblers make great cards." And with those words, the Gambler returned to the gaming table and prepared for the next game.

THE OPTIONS TRADER

J acob was a most curious and engaging boy with bright red hair and a quick smile. It was not unusual for his mother to find him talking with some traveler or merchant who was passing through their bustling village. After he finished helping his father in the fields or assisting his mother with the pigs and chickens, Jacob would often sit by the road where the travelers journeyed with their horses and mules, carrying supplies to and from the town. Jacob would begin by asking the weary merchants to join him in a drink of cool well water from the bucket he carried with him. After the traveler had drunk his fill, Jacob would start to chatter about life in the village and to ask about what it was like to journey from town to town, but eventually Jacob would ask the one question that was always on his mind, "What is it that you need in order to be successful in life?"

"My what a curious boy you are," began one robust merchant who was carting pots and pans on his two mules. "Most boys your age are interested in running in the fields or hunting birds and rabbits. Why is it that you ask such a serious question?"

"Kind sir, I have plenty of time to run and play, but I am interested in more than fun and games, and you seem like a man who has seen the world and understands the ways of success."

"Well," thought the merchant as he scratched his beard, "if I had to say one thing, I think I would say that hard work leads to success." But as he uttered those words, he could see the look of disappointment on Jacob's face. "Is there something wrong with hard work, young man, that you curl your lip and avert your eyes at my suggestion?"

"Oh no," cried Jacob, "I was rude to look away and of course I value your words of wisdom, but you see, I having been asking this question of many travelers and most tell me to work hard, respect my parents, and have patience. I do all of those things, but I was hoping for something else. I am searching for an answer that I have not heard before."

"Well, good luck my little friend. I hope you find the answer you seek and when you find it, I hope that it brings much success and happiness." And with those words, the merchant continued down the road with his mules and his wares to sell.

Time passed and Jacob continued to ask questions and to search for the key to the successful life. One crisp fall day, he was sitting as usual by the side of the road when an old man riding a most noble stallion suddenly appeared. The man drew his horse to a stop and began asking Jacob about the town and the people who lived there.

The two talked for quite a while and the old gentleman told Jacob of his travels in the most entertaining and clever way. Eventually, Jacob decided that he would ask this traveler his all-important question.

"Wise traveler," he began, "you have clearly seen much of the world and had many adventures. From your dress and your speech I gather that you have been quite successful and have accomplished much in your life. Please tell me, what is it that I will need in order to be successful in my life."

"Why that is simple," reflected the old man. "What you need to be successful in life is one thing that is really many things. You need options, yes indeed, options."

"What are options?" asked Jacob, eager to understand the full meaning of the old man's words.

"Infinite possibilities," mused the old man as he looked beyond the horizon and smiled.

The man was so certain and seemed so smart and successful that the young boy concluded he must indeed possess the secret to a successful life. "Options," Jacob repeated to himself, mulling the strange word over in his mind.

After his visit with the old traveler, Jacob vowed to collect as many options as he could. If he possessed infinite possibilities then surely whenever an opportunity for a new venture or an unexpected challenge arose Jacob would be prepared with just the right option. His success would be guaranteed.

From that moment on, every time Jacob was presented with a choice or a possibility for some action, he would write each of his options down on a separate slip of paper and place the papers in one of his pockets. After awhile, he had so many options that he did not have enough pockets to hold them all, so he took his options and placed them in a large burlap bag. And he carried his bag with him everywhere. After awhile, people in the village could not remember a time when Jacob was without his bag of options.

One day a group of men from a far off port arrived in the village loaded with silks and jewels and all manner of treasures. The villagers gathered around these travelers, eager for stories of their exploits and for tales of how they had found such an abundance of wealth. "Surely you are the most successful adventurers we have ever seen," cried the villagers. "Please tell us of your travels, so that we too might find treasure such as yours!"

The travelers told of sailing ships and adventures in faraway lands and then they made an offer to the villagers. "We are planning to sail in a few days to a land beyond the horizon that is said to be richer in wealth and more beautiful than any place we have been," explained the group's leader. "We need several strong young sailors to join us on our expedition. Each of those who come with us will receive a share of the riches we discover."

"Take me! Take me! Take me!" cried all of the young men who had assembled to hear the travelers' tales. Jacob was at the very front of the group and yelled the loudest of all.

"We can take many men with us," continued the leader. "But first we must arrange a contest to judge how fit you are to join our voyage. We will begin tomorrow morning just as the sun comes up. All who are interested in becoming part of our group must meet at the edge of town. When I give the signal you will begin a race that will take you all the way to the edge of the shore- line. All who reach the sea before the sun sets will be welcome to join our expedition."

Jacob could barely contain his excitement. At last all of his years of waiting and preparing would prove their value. His bag of options held all the skills and possibilities he would need to run the race faster than his comrades. He could hardly wait until the next morn- ing. Jacob knew that he would be on the starting line before the sun was up and, although his bag was quite heavy, he was certain that it contained all that he might need in order to be successful. "The old traveler was right," thought Jacob, "options are all you need if you are to be successful." And with that thought, he went off to get a good night's rest before the contest the next day.

As dawn broke, more than a hundred young men were lined up at the starting point. The leader gave the group his good wishes and then signaled them to begin the race. Jacob began at a good pace and ran through the woods and across the streams with confidence and optimism. Jacob knew this land well from years of walking the hills and talking to travelers and he was sure that he would reach the shoreline long before sunset. As the morning moved into afternoon, however, Jacob felt himself growing tired. The bag of options that he had strapped to his back felt hot and heavy.

"Perhaps I should put my bag of options down," he thought. "It would certainly be easier to run without them. I could just hide them here in the woods." But just as he was about to remove the bag of options, he had second thoughts. "How foolish of me to consider abandoning my options. After all, I have been collecting these possibilities for years and they hold the key to my success. How silly of me to even think about leaving them behind." And with that resolve, he poured more energy into his running and continued on his way.

As the evening approached, Jacob could just barely make out the edge of the shore. The race was almost over and while he would not be the first to reach the finish, Jacob would surely reach the end before the sun set. He was contemplating how relieved he would feel when the race was over, when all of a sudden he felt his legs fly out from under him. He had tripped over a rock and landed face down on the open field that stretched to the end of the race. As he was pulling himself up, Jacob noticed that his bag of options had ripped open as he fell. Little slips of options were now fluttering all around him, dancing in the wind like leaves in the fall. Jacob rose to his feet and quickly began retrieving his options. He had carried them all this way, and he was not about to let them escape now, just as he was so close to the finish line. If he hurried he would surely be able to collect his options and run to the shore before the sun set. But the breeze picked up and the options scattered in all directions. Jacob worked as fast as he could to collect his possibilities, but when he lifted his head to the horizon, he glimpsed the sight that he feared. The great ball of the sun was sinking slowly beneath the horizon.

TWO GIFTS

Deep in the Ural Mountains of Central Russia lived a powerful wizard. His fame for being able to foretell the future was so renowned that families brought him their newborn infants so that he might predict each child's future. One day in the late spring, a prominent family brought their baby daughter, Masha, to the home of the wizard. The baby's father was a rich farmer and the mother was not only beautiful, but was well known for being a talented musician. The new parents had great hopes for their first-born child.

The wizard sat quietly as the parents told of their daughter's birth and of their plans for her future.

"Your daughter will have a full life," intoned the wizard. "She will face many challenges, but she will triumph in the end."

"Is that all?" asked the disappointed and somewhat concerned parents, who had been hoping to hear that their daughter would marry a prince and become a famous songstress.

"No," said the wizard. "I will give Masha two gifts that will help her face the challenges that lie ahead." And with those words he entrusted the girl's mother with a small plain burlap bag fastened with a cord and containing something the wizard called "the Truth" and a small pair of glasses. The glasses had beautiful rose-colored lenses and the frames were encrusted with colorful stones and shiny pieces of metal resembling gold.

The parents returned to their home and put the gifts away in a small chest they kept in the attic. Despite all of their dreams and hard work, the years were not kind to the family. Several seasons of severe drought brought the family to the brink of financial ruin. Masha's father, who had been known for his wonderful sense of humor and his easy-going disposition, became sullen and withdrawn. Sometimes he would become angry, remembering the cryptic message of the wizard, and rage at Masha and her mother. Masha's mother, who had lost four other children in childbirth, no longer made music and only seemed happy when she was drinking from the wineskin she carried with her wherever she went.

All of this would have been unbearable for young Masha if it were not for a discovery she made one day while playing in the attic. Masha opened the chest where her gifts lay hidden and was immediately captivated by the beautiful glasses. At first she only amused herself by looking at the bright colored stones and the shiny metal, but one

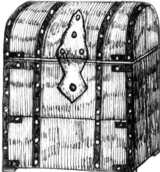

day she chanced to put on the glasses and made a most remarkable discovery. When she was wearing the glasses, the world appeared as she wanted it to be. The meager supper that her mother managed to put on the evening table looked like a holiday feast. Her mother's face shone and her now dull eyes once again twinkled with delight, and Masha's father's scowl turned into a huge playful grin. At first Masha only wore her glasses when she was feeling especially sad, but after awhile she took to wearing them most of the time. The world just looked nicer through the rose-colored glasses.

Just when the villagers thought that things could not get worse, a band of barbarians came down from the hills. They raped the women and stole what little property the villagers had left. The barbarian chief took the entire village as his prize and made all the people his prisoners. The village elders were distraught and pleaded with the chief on behalf of the villagers. At first the chief was outraged that the people would dare to approach him to ask for leniency, but then he agreed to a challenge. The villagers would be freed if they could produce "the Truth." If they failed, they and their descendants would be slaves to the chief and his tribe for three generations. Not knowing what else to do, the elders agreed to the chief's conditions.

When the elders told the people of the deal they had made, the men and women of the village cried out in horror and disbelief. "How will this help us?" they wailed. "We will never be able to meet the chief's challenge. Who among us knows what 'the Truth' is? And if we did know what the chief meant by 'the Truth,' how would we begin to find it?" Each of the villagers returned to his or her home to contemplate what to do.

Masha and her parents went back to their rundown home and began to prepare for the worst when Masha's father remembered that one of the wizard's gifts to Masha had been called something like "the Truth." Masha's mother sent her to the attic to see if the little burlap bag was still in the trunk. Masha ran upstairs, opened the trunk and peered inside, but she saw nothing. She returned to her parents and told them of her futile search.

"You cursed child," screamed her father. "Perhaps if you took off those silly glasses you wear all the time you might be able to see better."

"I will never take my glasses off," cried Masha. "The world is just too ugly without them."

Hearing that, her father became furious and struck Masha in the face, breaking her beautiful glasses and scattering the colored stones all over the floor. Masha scrambled to pick up the pieces of her broken glasses and retreated sobbing to a dark corner of the house. After her father calmed down, she snuck up to the attic to see if she might find some string to repair her glasses. This time, when Masha opened the chest, she saw the little bag of truth quite clearly. "How could I have missed it," she thought. "I searched every inch of this chest." Then Masha held the fragments of her broken glasses up to her eyes. Peering through the glasses, "the Truth" was no longer visible. It is a strange reality that you cannot see "the Truth" through colored glasses.

Masha grabbed the little bag and ran straight to the most respected elder in the village. At first he could not believe that a young girl had found "the Truth," but when he held the little bag he was convinced. Even the barbarian chief bowed before Masha and the bag of "Truth" she carried with her. With the discovery of "the Truth," the fortunes of the entire village changed. The rains came and the crops, which had been the source of the village's wealth, became even more bountiful than before.

The village elders asked Masha if they could have "the Truth" to display in a glass case at the local church along with other sacred objects. But Masha refused. "The Truth has been locked away in my attic for many years. It did none of us any good while it was hidden. The Truth deserves to be seen by all the people, so I will hang it out in the open on the branch of my favorite apple tree and then anyone who wants to can come and see and touch the Truth and make it their own."

Roots for Tanya

All of the women in Tanya's family were skilled gardeners. Her grandmother was a village wise woman whose potions and poultices were known to heal even the most troubling malady. And her aunt grew roses that graced the great hallway of the King's palace. Tanya just knew that when she grew up, she too would become a great tender of plants. Often when she visited with her grandmother she would ask, "When will I get my very own plants to grow?"

"Soon my dear child," her grandmother would always say. But never did her grandmother speak any words that might ease Tanya's impatience and her eagerness to learn the secrets of growing things. Then one day, shortly after Tanya's fifteenth birthday, her grandmother took her aside and said, "The time has come, Tanya, for you to take your place among the women in our family and become a gardener with great skill and power." Tanya was so excited she could barely control herself. She expected her grandmother to turn over a portion of the herb garden to her. Or perhaps she would be given a section of the flower garden for her very own. "No," she thought, "it will be something even more wonderful. My grandmother is going to give me a patch of land where I can grow anything I want."

As she followed her grandmother into the forest, Tanya could not stop smiling and humming to herself; she was so happy to be finally given her very own garden. When she and her grandmother had walked a long way into the woods, her grandmother knelt down beside a small plant with a thick stalk and branches of small feathery leaves. Her grandmother reached inside the gardening pouch that contained her tools and pulled out a small pruning knife. She then proceeded to cut a stem from the plant. The old woman carefully wrapped the cutting in a piece of damp burlap and handed it to Tanya.

"This is your very first project," she said with great authority and solemnity in her voice. "You must take this small cutting and help it to grow into a sturdy and strong plant. Place it in some good soil, water it regularly, and make sure it has enough sunlight. When you have grown this cutting well, come back to me and I will make you mistress of your very own garden."

Tanya hardly knew how to respond to her grandmother. She had been so sure that she would get her own garden right then. She had to turn her head to hide the tears that were welling up in her eyes.

"I know you are disappointed," said her grandmother gently, "but I would hardly be doing my job if I gave you a garden to care for before I was sure that you were ready for so big a responsibility.

Have patience, my dear, you will get your garden soon enough." And with that Tanya and her grandmother turned from the place where her grandmother had taken the cutting and returned along the path to the village.

Once she recovered from her disappointment, Tanya eagerly took up the task of growing her cutting into a strong and healthy plant. She did just as her grandmother had instructed. She took the cutting, placed it in a basket of soil, watered it, and set it in a corner of the garden where it would get just enough light. She knew just what to do since for years she had watched the women in her family start new plants in exactly this same way.

But Tanya was impatient for something to happen. After several hours, she gently lifted her cutting from the soil to see if any roots had grown yet. When she saw that there were none, she placed the cutting back in the basket and went about her other chores. But the next day Tanya once again became curious to see if her plant had taken root, and again she lifted the cutting from the basket. For each of the next ten days, Tanya went through the same process. She lifted her cutting from the basket, examined it for roots, saw none, and gently replaced the cutting in the soil.

Two weeks after she had taken her granddaughter into the forest, Tanya's grandmother came to inspect the progress of Tanya's plant. When she looked at the little stem in the basket, she shook her head in disappointment. "Why my dear child, your plant has not grown at all. In fact, it looks limp and quite sickly. I fear that it has not grown any roots and that it will soon die."

As she watched her grandmother walk away, Tanya sat down and began to cry, for she knew that her grandmother had spoken the truth. She had failed in her attempt to become a great gardener like the other women in her family. As she was sitting in the grass feeling sorry for herself, she was stunned to see a fat squirrel come up beside her and begin speaking in a small voice.

"Why are you crying, young lady?" he asked.

"Oh, I have made a big mess of everything. My grandmother gave me this cutting to grow and I have failed miserably. My poor little plant has just about died."

"Tell me exactly what you have done," demanded the squirrel.

"Each day, I have come to the garden, watered my cutting, made sure that it had enough sunlight, and lifted it from the soil to check to see if any roots had grown. Then I placed it back in the basket and went away."

"Well of course you have failed. I see why your plant has not grown!" declared the squirrel. "You have left out the most important part of being a gardener."

"I have?" puzzled Tanya, quite perplexed by the confident little squirrel.

"Now you must do exactly as I say and we will have your plant growing in no time. Each day, come to water your plant and turn it toward the sun and then do one more thing. After you have turned the basket, walk ten feet from the plant and say the following magical words, 'Little plant that I know, to make me happy you must grow.' After you have said these words, you must walk away from your plant and not return until the next morning. Follow these instructions exactly, and I promise that at the end of two weeks your little plant will be growing quite tall."

Although the squirrel's instructions seemed a little silly, Tanya decided to give his plan a try since she was quite without a plan of her own. Each day she came to the garden, watered her plant, turned the basket toward the sun, walked ten feet, and recited the magic words.

Two weeks passed and once again Tanya's grandmother came to inspect her plant. This time the old woman was quite pleased. "You have done a wonderful job, my dear. Your plant has grown two new shoots and seems well anchored in the soil. It will grow into a sturdy plant and you will grow into a great gardener."

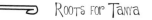
Tanya was very pleased with herself. She gave her grandmother a big hug, but she did not tell her about the magic words. Instead she went running to find her friend the squirrel.

"Oh, thank you! Thank you!" she cried, as she saw him nibbling on a small acorn in the corner of the garden. "The magic words did just as you said. My plant has grown tall and well. Now I will have a garden of my own and you can be sure I will always say the magic words."

The squirrel whose cheeks were already round with acorn meat, smiled a very big smile.

"Why my dear, I thought you would have guessed by now, the magic is not in the words; the magic is in the waiting."

Perfect Vision

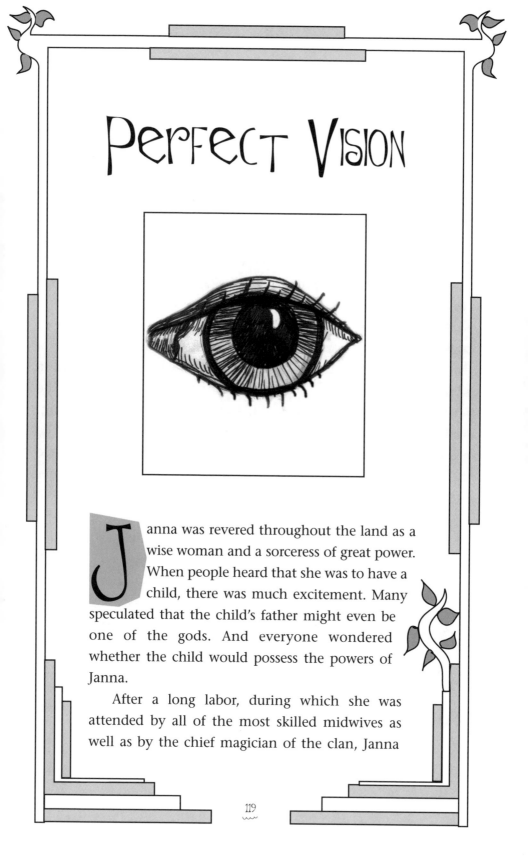

Janna was revered throughout the land as a wise woman and a sorceress of great power. When people heard that she was to have a child, there was much excitement. Many speculated that the child's father might even be one of the gods. And everyone wondered whether the child would possess the powers of Janna.

After a long labor, during which she was attended by all of the most skilled midwives as well as by the chief magician of the clan, Janna gave birth to a healthy baby girl. The child, who possessed the biggest and brightest brown eyes anyone could remember seeing, was called Karla in honor of one of the clan's most revered ancestors, and from the moment of her birth there were whispers among the members of the clan about whether she would possess Perfect Vision.

Karla was a happy child who seemed content no matter who held her or came to play with her. She smiled easily, but she also had a calm and serious side that caused many to comment that she seemed older than her years. Soon there were many knowing nods and winks as villagers and court attendants alike began to believe that Karla possessed powers like her mother's. Because she was the daughter of a wise woman, the very best teachers in the land were selected to supervise her education. And as she grew into a young woman, Karla learned all there was to know about the plants that healed and the rituals that soothed. She learned the ancient chants that had the power to change the direction of the wind and the force of the rain. And she learned to still the heart of her enemy and to make even the most raging beast respond to her gentle command. All of these things she learned, but still no one knew if she was one of the ones with Perfect Vision.

Throughout her childhood, Karla had often heard people whisper about something called Perfect Vision, but she herself had no idea what they meant by the words that were uttered in hushed tones and spoken with an averted gaze. Karla knew that she had been blessed with a keen sense of sight and that she could spot a rabbit running across the field at a great distance, but somehow she did not think that that was the kind of vision people were talking about. Sometimes when she was alone, she would wonder what Perfect Vision was and if she was indeed one of the chosen ones.

One day when Karla was sitting in the garden preparing for her daily lesson and playing with one of the stray cats that made its home under the dense shrubs, she decided to ask her most solemn teacher about Perfect Vision. "Master Magician," she began somewhat tentatively, "I have been a good student and I have tried hard to learn all that you have taught me. I have never questioned your insights, nor have I doubted your authority, but now I must ask you a question about something that you have never mentioned. Ever since I was a small child, people have whispered about Perfect Vision and have wondered if I possessed such powers, but no one has ever told me what those powers might be. I should so like to know so that I might be able to tell if I have the special powers."

"My dear child," began the magician, "you are correct that I have not spoken of Perfect Vision. It is a rare and unique power, possessed only by a few chosen ones in each generation. I cannot tell you what it is, because I myself do not possess the powers. I only know that if you are one of the ones with Perfect Vision you will know it soon enough. Now, let us begin your lesson and talk no more of this."

Karla was even more confused after her conversation with the magician than she had been before. Whatever this Perfect Vision was, it was certainly something mysterious. She would just have to wait and see.

One day Karla was watching as three of the younger children were playing by the edge of the cliffs that overlooked the sea. Karla thought to herself, "Those children are too close to the edge of the cliffs. If they stumble on some loose rocks, they will surely fall and hurt themselves."

"Be careful," she called out to the laughing children. "Those cliffs are dangerous!"

"Don't worry," called the children. "We are just having fun and you want to spoil our good time."

As Karla was just about to call out to the children one more time, the cliff gave way and the children tumbled into the sea. Villagers ran from all directions, crying and wailing as they realized what had happened. "If only someone could have seen how dangerous that cliff was," said one woman as she walked away shaking her head in disbelief.

"But I did see how dangerous it was," thought Karla. "I tried to warn the children, but they would not listen. They thought me a silly fool who just wanted to ruin their good time." Karla shuddered as she recalled the scene of the children falling onto the rocks below. Perhaps her awareness of the danger the children faced was somehow connected to what people meant by Perfect Vision.

Months passed and Karla put the incident with the children out of her mind. She went about her regular routine and tried not to think about Perfect Vision. And then one day a group of young men rode into the village and asked for volunteers to join them in an expedition to dig for gold in the distant hills. Each volunteer was to bring enough food and money to last for six months of exploring. The young men boasted of their previous successes and assured the eager volunteers that riches would soon be theirs. As Karla heard of the plans, she had a vision of her fellow villagers wandering lost in the hills, hungry and cold, their money stolen by the boastful young men.

"Don't go" she called out. "You do not know these men. They might very well be robbers who are planning to take your money and leave you stranded in the hills."

No sooner were the words out of her mouth than Karla was heckled and shouted down by her fellow villagers. "You worry too much Karla. We just want to have an adventure. You would stop us from making our fortune with your silly fears. Leave us alone Karla."

Karla hung her head and walked away. She knew she would never see some of her eager countrymen again. Now Karla knew what Perfect Vision was and she wasn't sure she liked it very much.

Several years passed and several more times Karla had visions of what was about to happen. Each time she told people what she saw and each time she tried to warn them to change their behavior and thus avoid almost certain disaster. She told the farmer not to plant in March but to wait until May because there was going to be a late frost, and she told the young maiden to find another beau because the man she was engaged to would surely make her cry. But each time people scorned Karla's advice. She was told that she worried too much or that she was too cautious. People criticized her for ruining their fun and putting a serious face on everything. After awhile people turned away when they saw Karla coming. They did not want to be told to stop this or to avoid that. It did not matter that her visions came true, people simply wanted to go about their lives and take their chances.

Karla grew sad and more isolated with the passing years. She did not like being the one to see what was going to happen, so one day she went to her old teacher and asked him what she should do with this Perfect Vision that allowed her to see things and know things but gave her no power to do anything about what she saw, except to tell people who seemed not at all interested in heeding her advice. The old magician listened to Karla's story and felt compassion for his former pupil who seemed so lonely and distressed.

"My dear Karla," he began, "I wish I knew how to help you, but since I myself do not possess Perfect Vision, my advice will be somewhat flawed. It seems, however, that your greatest distress comes from the reactions of your fellow villagers who do not want to benefit from your foresight. Perhaps all would be well if you simply kept your visions to yourself. Just because you see the future does not mean that you have to speak it."

"Of course," gushed Karla. "That is just the answer that I have been seeking. I will keep my visions to myself and all will be well. Thank you, thank you. Your advice is indeed wise."

Karla left the magician happier than she had been in a long time. And for a while she thought that all would be well. But soon after she visited the magician, Karla had another vision. This time she tried to keep her thoughts to herself, but the images she saw kept forcing themselves into her consciousness. Just keeping them to herself did not make them go away. She tried to keep her own counsel, but finally the visions were so powerful that she found herself telling what she saw to anyone who would listen. The magician's advice had failed. She would have to find a better way to deal with her Perfect Vision.

After much thought, Karla decided to seek the counsel of the wisest sorceress in the land. Surely the Old One would know how to make this Perfect Vision go away. Karla traveled over the hills to the temple where the Old One lived and worked her spells. As Karla approached the sorceress, she thought about what she was going to say. She would ask the Old One if she could take the gift of Perfect Vision and give it back.

"Most revered sorceress," began Karla. "I am the daughter of Janna and have been schooled in the ways of the wise ones. I have come to you to ask about my Perfect Vision. I have the gift of perfect sight and I would like to know how I might give this gift back. You see, it is not so easy to possess Perfect Vision."

"My dear child, I know all too well what it is like to have Perfect Vision. You see, I have lived my life possessing the very same power and I too have had to find a way to live with this awesome vision. But before I tell you of my experience and that of others who were chosen to have Perfect Vision, I must ask you one question. What makes you think that Perfect Vision is a gift?"

The Wizard's Message

It was a warm summer day, and Tran had been climbing in the hills near his village for many hours before he stumbled on the remains of what looked like an old cottage. It appeared as if the roof had collapsed a long time ago, and the walls of the cottage were now overgrown with vines and quite a variety of weeds. Known for his curiosity, Tran could not resist the opportunity to explore, especially since he did not recall having seen these exact remains before during his frequent climbs into the hills. As he poked through the rubble, uncovering a piece of broken pottery or shard of colored glass, Tran recalled stories of an old wizard who had lived in these hills a long time before. "Perhaps I have found the wizard's cottage," he thought. "Who knows what magical charms might be hidden beneath all this mess." And with that thought, he began to dig through the rubble with more determination.

After many hours, Tran grew tired and decided to stop and rest. As he prepared to stretch out under a tree, he felt something sharp sticking out from the ground. With a little digging, Tran managed to remove a large piece of stone, almost like a tablet. As he examined the object, Tran was surprised to see how smooth the surface was despite years of being buried and forgotten. Holding the heavy stone in both of his hands, Tran observed that it bore an inscription, carefully carved in a script that his people had not used for many years. Remembering the lettering he had been taught as a boy, Tran read the cryptic message: NEVER GIVE UP. "Was that all," he wondered as he turned the stone over to see if there was more. But he found nothing, only those three words.

At first Tran was disappointed with his discovery. He had hoped that the tablet would hold the clue to some magic charm or perhaps a map that would lead him to buried treasure, but as he repeated the three words over and over in his mind, Tran became more and more excited. "I have discovered the true wisdom of the wizard," he thought. "These three words hold the key to success in all things. I will follow the wizard's message from now on." And with that promise, Tran replaced the wizard's stone in the soft earth and prepared to head back down the mountain.

The summer turned to fall and Tran went about his normal business, harvesting the last of his crops and preparing to take them to market in the village. He thought little of the wizard's message although he had copied the three words onto a piece of parchment that he kept in a pouch around his waist along with his other valuables.

As the winter drew to a close, Tran decided that the time had come for him to find a wife. For years he had admired the shy older daughter of his neighbor, but Tran had never had the courage to say more to the young woman than "Good day" or "Good evening." "How shall I approach her?" he thought. "She is so lovely and I am just an awkward farmer. She will surely have no interest in a suitor like me." And then Tran remembered the wizard's message, NEVER GIVE UP, and he began to devise a plan to court the young woman. Tran sent her gifts and serenaded her with poetry. At first she avoided Tran and refused to answer his many entreaties, but after several weeks she grew intrigued with this suitor who seemed so determined to win her affections. The two began to take long walks and to talk of their plans and dreams for the future, and within a year Tran and the young woman, Ling, were married. Tran was most pleased with his new bride, but he was especially excited to see the power of the wizard's message. "Before I found the wizard's stone," he thought, "I would have abandoned my courtship of Ling and now I have the most wonderful wife. I am a lucky man to know the wizard's secret. I will let those three words guide me in all things."

Years passed and the couple gave birth to three healthy sons. Tran and his wife continued to farm the land, but every year at planting time they struggled with clearing the fields of the many rocks that shifted down from the mountains with the winter snows. "If only I could find a way to clear these rocks more quickly," Tran complained to his wife, "then we could clear twice as much land and grow more wheat. With a larger harvest I am sure we would become quite rich. But I am afraid it will take a smarter man than I to invent some way to clear these fields."

"Nonsense!" declared his wife. "Remember the wizard's message. It has never failed us before, and I am sure if you keep trying, you will find a way to make our harvest more bountiful." Ling felt completely free to invoke the wizard's message in her mild reprimand of her

husband since the wizard's words had now become the guiding principle for the whole family.

Tran and his sons spent hours each day trying various contrap-
tions that might solve their problem and after many attempts, they
did indeed invent a plow that tossed the heavier rocks aside while
plowing the field in perfectly straight rows. With their invention, the
family was able to plant and harvest more wheat and very quickly
the family fortunes grew. Tran and Ling and their three sons were
now among the richest people in the entire valley.

Years passed and the family enjoyed the benefits of their hard
work. In the evenings Tran and Ling would talk of how lucky they
had been to find the wizard's message and how satisfied they were
with their lives. "How could we possibly want for more?" Tran was
often heard asking to no one in particular.

Then one day a traveler appeared in the village telling stories of
treasure buried high on the highest mountain. The villagers listened
intently as the man told of his own attempts, as well as those of
many others, to find the treasure. "If so many know of this treasure,"
asked Tran, "then why is it that no one has successfully brought the
treasure down the mountain?"

"You ask a wise question, friend," replied the man. "The treasure
is buried high on a part of the mountain that is accessible only in
winter. Whoever seeks the treasure must travel through snow and ice
and persevere despite difficult conditions. I guess all of us who have
tried gave up before we reached the goal."

"Of course," thought Tran to himself because he did not want to
share his plans with the rest of the villagers, it is the wizard's message
once again. "I will seek the treasure and succeed where others have
failed because I know the secret: NEVER GIVE UP." With that thought,
Tran smiled to himself and began to formulate his plan for discovering
the treasure.

After weeks of preparing for his journey, Tran set off to climb the
mountain with the blessings of his wife and sons who were convinced

that he would return with great wealth. The first part of his climb went quite easily, and Tran felt confident that he would soon be a rich man. After almost two weeks of climbing higher and higher, Tran came to a bridge made of pure ice. "Certainly this bridge is too difficult to cross," he thought. "I will just sit here and rest for a bit." And then he heard the words of the wizard's message sounding softly inside his head. "Of course, this is the test," he reasoned. "This must be where others turn back; I will cross the bridge and find the treasure."

Tran had almost crossed the narrow bridge of ice when the snow and wind began to blow fiercely. "Hold on," Tran told himself. "You are almost there, just a few more steps." But as he placed his foot on what he thought was solid ground, the snow beneath his boots gave way. Tran reached for something solid, but grabbed only frozen air as he fell into the deep and jagged crevasse below.

As the weeks and months passed, Ling and her sons grew more and more worried that something had happened to Tran. If he followed the plan he had shared with them, he should have been home just as the spring snows were beginning to melt. It was now almost planting time and Tran was still not back in the valley. With each passing day, the family grew more and more concerned that Tran would never return. One evening, Tran's oldest son proposed to the family that he form a search party and go up the mountain to discover what had become of his father. "We cannot all leave home at planting time, so I will take three of my comrades and go into the hills. If father is lost in the mountains we will help him home and if he has met with some terrible accident, we will bring home his body to be buried here in the valley with our ancestors."

"Go, my son," said Ling softly. "Your plan is a good one and I wish you Godspeed. Remember to follow the words of the wizard and NEVER GIVE UP until you find your father."

Tran's son and his friends began their search the very next morning. They climbed high into the foothills and were about to turn up a steep path leading to the tallest mountain when one of their party noticed a strange shape at the bottom of one of the steep crevasses. "Look over there," he called to his companions. "There is something at the bottom of that gorge that could be the body of a man." The friends looked over the edge of the crevasse and silently began their descent to what all feared would be the broken body of Tran. As the young men got closer it became apparent that the twisted shape was indeed all that was left of Tran's body. His son approached the body first and lovingly said a prayer over the corpse of his father while the others waited. He then wrapped the body in a large leather sheet he had hoped never to need but had brought just in case. "Come," he called. "Help me carry my father home."

As the men began to lift the body, one of them noticed a small piece of parchment that must have been clutched in the dead man's hand. "What is that?" asked Tran's son as he reached for the paper. There, written in his father's handwriting, was the wizard's message: NEVER GIVE UP. As he held up the paper tears welled in the young man's eyes.

"What is it?" asked one of his friends. "It is the wizard's message," replied the son. "It was the principle by which my father guided his life and the fortunes of our family."

"Let me see that," demanded another member of the group who had been silent up until now. "That is not the wizard's full message. Indeed, it is only half of the wisdom he taught."

"How can that be?" exclaimed Tran's son. "My father found this message many years ago when he discovered the cottage of the wizard overgrown with weeds and shrubs."

"He must have overlooked the second half of the message," insisted the man who spoke with such certainty. "The wizard was a dear friend of my great grandfather and I learned his wisdom from his own lips."

"Pray then," began Tran's son with a hint of dread in his voice. "Tell me the full message of the wizard."

"NEVER GIVE UP," began the young man in a deliberate voice, "UNLESS THE QUEST IS HOPELESS."

Speak to Me

Josie's mother, Lyla, was known throughout their large but close-knit community as a very wise woman. Whenever family members or neighbors needed advice or guidance, they would call on Lyla, who would listen and give good counsel. Many wondered how it was that Lyla seemed to know just the right thing to say to each person when their concerns were all so different. Lyla had no special training as a counselor or an advisor, but she spoke with a clarity that made people stop and listen.

"How is it that you understand so much, mother?" Josie would often ask during one of their many long talks. "I speak from my heart, daughter. If you listen well, your own heart will speak and tell you all you need to know of truth," Lyla would respond. Josie was not quite sure what her mother meant or whether she had the power to listen as her mother did, but Josie was always comforted knowing that as long as her mother was alive, Lyla would help her figure out what to do.

As the years passed, Josie began to worry just a little about what she would do when the time came for Lyla to pass from this life to the next. "Mother, how will I know what to do when you are gone?" she would ask. "Don't be silly, my darling daughter," Lyla would respond. "You too are wise. Look at all you have accomplished. You have a loving family of your own and you have traveled to many countries and spoken with women far wiser than I."

"No, no," insisted Josie, sounding like the little girl she had not been for many years. "You don't understand. I need to be able to talk with you. What will I do when you are gone?" Lyla tried to reassure her daughter, but no manner of reasoning seemed to quiet Josie's anxiety. "Please mother, you are wise and you have powers far greater than most women. Teach me how I might be able to speak with you even after you are gone."

For years, Josie had observed Lyla sitting, from time to time, in silent reverie, speaking from her heart to the spirits of ancestors long gone. "I know that you have found a way to speak with your mother; you have told me so. Please teach me so that I might always be able to speak with you even when you no longer walk this earth." Although she tried to resist Josie's pleas at first, Lyla eventually gave in to her daughter's request. "My dear daughter, you are silly to believe that I have some magic formula for speaking with the dead. My prayers are very private, but if you insist I will tell you what I do. When I feel the need for my own mother's wisdom, I sit very quietly and concentrate with the core of my being. Sometimes I can feel her presence, and I feel comforted and at peace." Josie listened intently to her mother's description and then asked, "If I concentrate as you do, mother, will I be able to hear your voice and know your wisdom?" "I can make no promises," Lyla responded, "but I will do my best to guide you and love you always." Josie smiled and wrapped her arms around her mother's broad shoulders.

More years passed, and Josie herself grew into a wise and respected woman in the community. She still sought Lyla's counsel, although she relied on Lyla less for everyday advice. Josie never forgot the conversation she had had with her mother years before, however, and she became convinced that her mother's voice would never leave her. Surely if anyone could cross the ineffable boundaries of space and time, Lyla and her love for Josie would.

One day, after a brief illness, Lyla closed her eyes for the last time. Josie and all her brothers and sisters and most of the community came to say good-bye and honor the woman who had advised and comforted so many of them. Josie's sorrow for her mother was deep, but she busied herself with preparations for the funeral and by offering comfort to the other mourners who came from all around. And for a time after the burial, Josie could hardly believe that Lyla was really gone. Her mother's spirit was so strong that Josie kept expecting to see Lyla or hear her mother's voice as she went about her daily routine.

As time passed, Josie found herself missing her mother more, not less. She missed their long talks and her mother's strong opinions. She missed Lyla's warm smile and her soft caress. And she missed the sweet cookies that Lyla served every day at teatime. "If only I could talk to my mother," she thought with a heavy sigh, and then she remembered her conversation with Lyla so long ago.

"Of course," she said out loud to herself, "I will sit and concentrate and surely Lyla will come and speak to me." And so she prepared a special spot for her anticipated "visit" with her mother. Josie wrapped herself in a shawl her mother had knitted, sat in her favorite chair, and inhaled the sweet aroma of Lyla's own blend of spice tea. And as Josie thought about her mother, she waited, and she waited, and she waited. But no voice made itself known. "Where are you

Mother?" she called. "Please speak to me. I am your daughter, Josie, and I need to hear your voice yet again." But no matter how she pleaded or how long she waited, no voice came. She tried her experiment a few more times, each time with less confidence and always with the same result. No sound from Lyla.

"Perhaps I am doing something wrong," she thought to herself. "Perhaps the dead do not communicate through words. Perhaps their way is different from ours. Perhaps my mother will give me some sign that she is with me still." So Lyla began to look for signs in the shapes of the clouds, in the calls of the birds, in the bubbling sound of the evening stew. She looked for evidence of her mother's voice, but she found none, and after awhile Josie stopped believing that she would ever hear Lyla's voice again.

Time passed, and Josie turned her attention to raising her own quite large family. She was especially close to her oldest daughter, who had also been a favorite granddaughter of Lyla's. The young girl was quite an accomplished musician and one summer was invited to give a recital before a large audience of visitors at the town hall. Josie listened with pride as her daughter performed with grace and skill. As she was congratulating her daughter after the performance, Josie found herself saying, "Your grandmother would be so proud of you. I know just what she would have said if she had been here to hear you play." And with those words Josie recited a prayer that she had often heard her mother say on special occasions. Her daughter beamed upon hearing the familiar words. "Why, you sound just like Grandmamma when you say that," she exclaimed. "Do I now?" mused Josie. "How nice."

Weeks passed and Josie did not think much about her daughter's comment at the recital. Then one day she was shopping at the big open-air market that occupied the center of town when she heard herself saying to the baker, "I am a good customer and you do indeed bake the best bread in town, but you'll not get my money for bread that is a day old." The baker looked surprised, for it was unlike Josie to speak so boldly. As she saw his response, Josie laughed to herself.

She could almost hear her mother's many conversations with the town's merchants echoing at the back of her mind.

Josie was not sure what to make of her experience at the market, but she put it out of her mind as she prepared for the visit of her cousin whom she had not seen since Lyla's death. Her cousin's visit was a joyous occasion because the two had been almost like sisters growing up. While the two women sat over a pot of tea and talked, Josie brought out a plate of sweet cookies just as her mother had done on so many occasions. As the two ate and talked, Josie's cousin asked what she had learned over the last several years since Lyla's death. Josie replied simply and without thinking, "I have learned that life is short and we must enjoy every day we are given." Before the words were even out of her mouth, Josie realized that she was repeating a comment she had heard her mother make a thousand times before.

"Those are wise words," responded her cousin. "You sound just like Lyla when you say that."

"It's funny you should say that," replied Josie. "I have been saying and doing more and more things that I know Momma would have said. I still have one regret though. I have not heard my dear mother's voice over these many years. I had so hoped that she would find a way to speak to me from beyond."

"How odd of you to say that," remarked Josie's cousin, "for when I am with you I feel as if I am in the presence of Lyla herself. You sound so much like her that I feel that she is speaking to me when I hear you talk."

Josie looked startled at her cousin's words and then smiled to herself. "Thank you Mother," she thought, "I guess you *have* been there all along, I just needed to learn how to listen to your voice."

Myth Commentary

For many readers, the stories in this collection will need no additional commentary. The reader will have found, or not found, personal meaning in the stories. Some stories will resonate with one's inner voice, while others will not. And some stories will be solely engaging, but not deeply meaningful. Such is the nature of stories.

But for other readers, the stories alone will not be sufficient. They will want to engage in a dialogue about the stories, wanting to know what a particular story was intended to mean. For these readers, I offer the following commentary, not to suggest that I have the true meaning of the stories, because the true meaning lies in each individual reader's response to the fables, but merely for the purpose of sharing my own thoughts as I wrote or read each of the twenty-four stories.

The Alchemist

So often we hope for some magical intervention to change our lives and bring us instant happiness and lasting contentment and peace. Some of us may even be tempted to suspend any constructive activity that might bring about a significant change in our life circumstances while we wait for some magical change that will finally arrive and make things just right. The young man in the story believed in a miracle, but actually transformed himself through hard work, work that was at times boring, at times routine, and at times slow going. And while the work was not glamorous or exciting, it was work that needed to be done. So too, many individuals discover that the work they do in their lives and in their personal growth, however stressful and at times tedious it might be, is the real magic that brings about true change and enduring emotional reward.

Better Safe Than Sorry

Whenever we feel confronted with danger, it makes sense to protect ourselves. And that protection may well take the form of erecting barriers that separate us from the rest of the world. For some, however, those barriers become impenetrable walls that enclose us in a world of isolation and limitation. It is especially true that when children grow up in violent and abusive homes, they cling to any source of safety regardless of how costly and ultimately limiting it might be. After awhile, the path of safety may become a way of life and we may forget that there was a time when we gladly took more risks and ventured further afield in order to fully experience the world. Finding a healthy balance between the need for safety and the drive toward openness and exploration is a challenge for all of us and is particularly difficult for those who have experienced profound loss or trauma.

The Burden

We all learn to accommodate the burdens that life experience has placed on us. We bend with the weight of loss and abuse and disappointment. And we are often quite adept at constructing a life around some debilitating symptom or some great internal pain. After awhile we may become so good at adapting that we, too, forget that we are carrying something that greatly limits our choices and opportunities. When we finally become aware of the limitations imposed by years of unhappiness and distress, we may believe that the road to recovery is too steep to climb. We may even believe that it will be almost impossible to be free of our burdens. But, like the young man in the story, we may find that all it takes is the courage and the will to lay the burden down. Some changes require years to effect and some require merely placing our stick upon the pile and walking away.

The Cave of Truth

On the path of recovery, we all look for mentors, guides, and counselors whose wisdom and knowledge might make the task of healing somewhat easier. We want these wise people to tell us what we need to do in order to feel better. And often they can do just that. We can benefit from the advice and counsel of others and we can certainly profit from knowing people who have successfully struggled with demons and recovered. Yet at some point in each individual's journey the time comes for discovering a truth that is unique to oneself. We must each find the things that make our own lives meaningful and, although we may borrow from others, we must ultimately find the path that is genuinely our own. As difficult as it sometimes is to accept, there are some things that each of us must learn for ourselves.

The Contest

There is no such thing as universal happiness. What makes one individual glow with contentment may seem tedious and boring to another. Yet, despite the fact that we may know full well that each individual must seek his or her own happiness, we still look to others to give us the formula for a happy life. We read advice columns and buy self-improvement books in search of some one-size-fits-all prescription for happiness. Each speaker in the story has his or her own path to happiness, and when the King realizes that the paths are as different as the people in his kingdom, he understands an essential truth: each of us must find our own formula for contentment, and although we may borrow from others, we must ultimately choose that which fits our own unique self.

The Diver

Each time we approach a challenge, we ask ourselves "Am I up to the job?" We want to know if we are capable of taking on a new responsibility or if we are ready to push ourselves to the next level of accomplishment. Often we look to others—teachers, mentors and friends—to guide us in our decision making. And frequently their counsel helps us to make the right choice. But sometimes there are decisions that cannot be guided by another. Part of being ready for a new challenge or a new relationship is having access to one's internal voice. We know that we are ready not because someone else tells us that we are, but because we know it intuitively and have come to trust our intuitions. Paradoxically, there are times when needing someone to tell us that the time is right for a particular move means unequivocally that the time is not.

The Gambler's Lesson

So often when things do not go our way, we find ourselves complaining that life is not fair. We imagine that there are others who have an easier time of living than we do. And we are certain that some fortunate group of "lucky" ones do not share our tribulations. During these times of lament and self pity, it does not occur to us that even those we deem fortunate have had their share of heartache. Why is it then, if each of us must contend with our share of pain, that some appear to live problem-free lives while others rage against the capriciousness of the universe? Perhaps, as the gambler tells his reluctant pupils, the trick really is in how we play the cards we are dealt. It certainly takes little skill to play a winning hand. In fact, some cards are so good that even a novice could not misplay the hand. Conversely, some cards are so bad that even the most skilled player cannot turn them into a winning hand. But the real skill in both cards and life comes from how we play the average hand, the hand that is not an automatic winner or a sure loser. The hand with some good cards and some losers requires that we see its possibilities and play with all the skill and determination we have.

The Gift of Choices

Decisions are difficult for most of us, but they are especially hard for individuals who have sustained a significant loss, betrayal, or trauma in childhood. In an abusive or dysfunctional family, a child often grows up in a world in which someone else makes all or most of the decisions. The child is given no chance to decide for him or herself, so it becomes silly to think of oneself as a person who has the authority and the skill to make decisions. As adults, many of us turn over decision making power to anyone and everyone. Rather than seeming like opportunities, decisions feel like unscalable mountains. So instead of even beginning the climb, we merely sit and look up at the mountain and wait.

Sometimes we have the unfortunate experience of making a big decision that appears to have disastrous consequences. We may then become even more tentative about future decisions. We say to ourselves "What if I make a mistake and something worse happens? Better not to decide at all." But as Wide Eyes learns in the story, one cannot help but decide. We make decisions every day in so many little ways, and there is no way to know for certain what constitutes a big decision or a small one. The fork in the road may be inconsequential or it may represent the decision that determines the rest of one's life. Just as there are no small decisions, there is no way to avoid deciding. We make a choice when we decide "not to decide." And as Wide Eyes learns, we use our choices even when we try not to.

Gold and Silver

Whether we are entrusted with nurturing a family, a business, a community, or our own inner life, each of us must find a way to provide care and support and to establish the optimum conditions for growth and development. Do we nurture by being overly responsible and making sure that we keep all harm at bay, or do we provide support by teaching ourselves and those around us how to find joy and fulfillment in everyday tasks? Clearly, some balance of the two choices is called for. Without an awareness of the dangers that threaten us and those around us, we may fail to take needed precautions. Unfortunately, when individuals have experienced repeated trauma or abuse, they may focus too heavily on preparing for what can go wrong without attending to the pleasure that awaits in everyday experience. Caring for ourselves, in particular, demands that we find ways to enjoy the life that we have created. But again, play at the expense of responsibility may jeopardize the things and people we value most. Many have suffered because those entrusted with their care were more concerned with having a good time than with providing safety and support. As with many things, the answer often lies in some creative combination. We need to find ways to be both responsible and joyful if we are to truly nurture our relationships and our creations, whether they are gardens or families or public enterprises or the very personal growth that takes place inside each of us.

Inktomi

Oh how we long to be different! Whether it is some minor self-improvement or a major transformation, we invest much time, energy, and money in trying to be other than we are. No one would argue that some attempt at self-improvement is often necessary for any process of growth and change. We feel dissatisfied with who we are, we long to be different, and sometimes we begin a process of healthy transformation. Unfortunately, as was the case with Inktomi, the longing to be different can be so powerful that it obscures the virtues we already possess. We may also be so eager for change that we fail to notice the price that we must pay for certain changes. We may also fail to notice that what works for one person may not work quite as well for us. So often many of the strengths and gifts we look for outside ourselves are virtues and talents we already possess, if only we have the wisdom to notice them before it is too late.

Just One String

Loss is one of the most powerful human experiences and repeated loss can be devastating. When we lose a special relationship, a cherished possession, or a valued job we can imagine that we have lost an essential part of ourselves, something we cannot recover. Yet, no matter how much we lose, we cannot lose the essential thread of who we are. Memory remains the connection to our past and even in a life that has been battered by pain and trauma, there are some memories of joy and contentment. The very act of remembering can be a source of strength and triumph over the losses and assaults of the past. Recognizing that we remain ourselves, no matter what the world takes away from us, can be the first step in learning to live with the losses that inevitably come in every life.

A Language of Your Own

We each begin with the ability to speak what is on our minds. Children, in fact, are infamous for saying what they think with little regard for the social consequences. Yet somewhere along the way, in our desire to please others or to fit in with our peers, we may find that we silence the dialogue with our own inner voice. The estrangement from our own true voice may be so extreme that we even find ourselves unsure what we really think and feel and looking to others to tell us what we are supposed to believe. The struggle to regain connection with one's inner voice may be particularly arduous. Sometimes a period of silence or stillness is required to allow the thoughts and feelings that live inside us to emerge clearly from the din of the noise around us. It requires courage to speak from the heart and to risk the disapproval of others who want us to talk their language. But, as with the girl in the story, the only chance we have for true communication is to speak simply and clearly from the heart.

The Most Evil Man in Town

As we are growing up, we all promise ourselves that we will never be like the people in our lives who have caused us pain. We vow never to scream and holler the way Dad did, or never to become emotionally withdrawn the way Mom was. We will be different, we tell ourselves, and implied in that promise is the belief that we will be better. And when we make that promise we are sincere in our intentions, but often, without our awareness, in small almost imperceptible increments, we find ourselves saying the very words, doing the same things that we swore we would not. How to avoid replicating the sins of the past becomes a central mission in any recovery process. It may well require a special vigilance to learn from the past without repeating it because by bringing the painful dynamics of childhood into the present, we remain the prisoner of the old abuses long after we think we have moved on.

The Options Trader

Without options and choices in our lives we feel limited and even trapped. Yet is it ever possible to have too many options? Indeed, is it possible to have so many options that one is actually paralyzed into indecision, burdened by the weight of too many choices? While we are collecting our options, evaluating the benefits of one choice against the merits of several others, we may find that we miss out on some of the joys of everyday living. We strive for one more credential; we compete for one more bonus; we scheme to have one more date. And each time we tell ourselves that this additional opportunity will open the door to all that we seek in order to be truly happy. Yet while we are collecting and analyzing our options, real opportunities for adventure or just plain living may be overlooked. We need choices, of course, but ultimately, we need to be able to make the best use of the choices we have.

Perfect Vision

One of the most difficult struggles is to see the world with clarity and honesty. We all want to believe that our decisions are sound and our choices wise, and we often find a way to ignore those signs that suggest otherwise. The people in our lives who try to tell us that we are about to make a mistake may seem like our worst enemies rather than our best friends. Yet for each of us, genuine growth and change require that we recognize the truth that sits before us, even if it means that we will have to put aside an activity or a relationship that satisfies us for the moment. Still, seeing the truth should not mean that we live in fear and anxiety. Sometimes the answer to a healthy life lies in seeing reality, making adjustments, and then continuing to find ways to be engaged in the world.

The Pot of Misery

Painful memories have a way of lingering long after we think we have put them to rest. At times, everyday events trigger a return to past hurts. Sometimes we intentionally revisit the past to see if old arrows still have the power to wound us. Often we search for some way to still the voices of despair and discontent permanently. We hope that through meditation, therapy, or some type of self-exploration we can banish the demons of the past forever. One of the hardest lessons to learn is that the demons remain part of us forever, forming an essential part of who we are and who we have become. Just as our strengths and our triumphs are there to sustain us, our traumas are there to remind us of how far we have come. We can, however, learn how to tame and contain the worst of the nightmares. A caged beast, after all, may still growl occasionally, but it no longer has the power to attack and cause harm.

The Puzzler

"To know or not to know," that is the question that faces many of us as we struggle with the demons of the past. We have come to believe that a reconstruction of the past is necessary in order for any true recovery to occur. And certainly, complete amnesia about the past leaves us feeling without a stable foundation on which to build a future identity. Yet many have uncovered realities about the past that make living in the present painful and at times almost impossible. How much to uncover about a traumatic and torturous past is something that each individual must decide for him or herself in pursuit of recovery. There is no solution that applies universally to all; rather, the answer lies in the heart of each individual.

Roots for Tanya

Waiting is difficult for all of us, especially if we have lived a lifetime with pain and despair. When an individual who has suffered a great deal finally makes a decision to change, perhaps by entering into formal treatment or by beginning a process of self-exploration, she may be so eager to see results that she has little patience with the slow process of growth and change. Like the young girl in the story, some of us wear ourselves out by asking ourselves and others "Have I changed yet? Have I changed yet?" The disappointment when change does not come rapidly may be enough to drive some of us from the process of growth and self-discovery, feeling either that we have failed or that the process of change has let us down like so many other things have in the past. The willingness to respect the slow process of growth is one of the keys to overcoming the horrors of the past.

The Silver Flute

The work of recovery is just that—work. Individuals who have gone through the healing process know there is much to be done and mastered before one can emerge from the other side of despair and disillusionment. Yet many of us enter recovery services seeking a miracle. For some individuals, the wait to seek help has been so long that when they finally reach the point of seeking services, they feel desperate and impatient for things to change. Others have grown up believing that their own actions have little if any impact on what eventually happens to them. Consequently they believe that change will only occur if some divine presence grants them a miracle. And still others feel that it is sufficient to say that they are entering a recovery program. They sign up for services but fail to participate regularly. At the end of the treatment program, they hope to have been healed even though they have not been present for the groups and sessions and support that are a necessary part of change and transformation. And, like the young man in the story, there are some who believe that there must be another, easier, way to achieve the sought-after goal.

The good news and the bad news about recovery is that it requires work and commitment and perseverance. At last, individuals can direct their own recovery; they can have the power and the control to make things change. A man or woman can go as far as he or she chooses down the road of repair. But with that power comes responsibility and the sometimes difficult and tedious struggles that accompany any human growth.

Speak to Me

How do we deal with the loss of someone we love? Of course we mourn and we remember. We may become angry and at times despondent as we long for the familiar touch, the knowing smile. We may spend hours reminiscing, but each of us tries, in his or her way, to hold on to the essence of the person who is gone. Some families establish a shared ritual that commemorates the life of the one who has passed on. Others find some way to keep a favorite interest alive by giving to charity or continuing to perform certain tasks. Certainly one way that families hope to keep the spirit of a loved one alive is

by nurturing the next generation. Often a new addition to the family will be given the name or nickname of one who has recently died
and whose memory is cherished. But what many of us find, sometimes quite by accident, is that we keep alive the spirit of a beloved
ancestor or a special friend or companion by incorporating into ourselves some quality or mannerism or trait of that person. The person
never leaves us when we see some aspect of them in us.

The Travelers

What constitutes the "good life?" How we each wish we knew. So
often we evaluate one person's life by standards that make sense for
somebody else. One person's joy or comfort is another person's lost
island. In working with women and men in recovery or when talking with friends, family, or lovers, it is sometimes difficult to see the
world through the eyes of the other. Perspective, the ability to stand
in someone else's shoes and look out, is essential if we are to be part
of another's healing journey. There are few, if any, right answers
about how to live the "good life." We must be willing to entertain
many different paths to recovery and healing. And as individuals we
must learn to respect our own view of what makes us happy rather
than trying to find our happiness in another person's vision.

The Twenty-Four Carat Buddha

We have all heard the axiom, "trick me once, shame on you; trick me
twice, shame on me." And we have all promised ourselves that we will
not make the same mistake twice. Yet we may regrettably find ourselves returning to people or circumstances that have hurt or disappointed us before. In part, we want to believe that our colleagues and
friends are sincere and honest and that a promise made will be a
promise kept. We also like to think that we are shrewd enough to
avoid repeating the same mistakes. At best, however, a repeated mistake leaves us feeling hurt and disappointed. At worst, it may result in

dangerous victimization. When a woman returns to an abusive part-ner, for example, she may jeopardize her very safety. As much as we may want to give people a chance to change, not learning from past mistakes can be dangerous business.

Two Gifts

Denial is a powerful barrier to seeing the truth. Often we struggle to be honest with ourselves and with others about what we see and what we believe. But the truth is sometimes painful, and we may feel compelled to wear the glasses of denial just to survive from day to day. Individuals who have experienced profound loss, abuse, or disappointment at the hands of caregivers may find that without the glasses of denial they are unable to cope. Rose-colored glasses sometimes make an abusive child-hood bearable. Unfortunately those same glasses obscure the truth, and when an individual reaches adulthood, she or he may find the truth hardly recognizable. It takes great courage to voluntarily put the lies and distortions aside and stare bare-eyed at the truth; yet that is just what survivors must do if they are to heal from the scars of abuse.

The Wizard's Message

Perseverance and determination are clearly among the keys to suc-cess. Often we miss out on an opportunity because we give up too quickly. Yet persisting in a foolhardy or hopeless cause can be as problematic as walking away too soon. Especially in the world of rela-tionships, we find ourselves having to negotiate the delicate balance between abandoning a relationship prematurely just because there are difficulties and persisting in a relationship way beyond the point that makes sense. We may even find ourselves so committed to see-ing something through to its conclusion that we become more invested in "not being a quitter" than we are in a successful outcome. We often find that the decision of when to persist and when to back away is best made when we have all of the relevant information.

Questions for Discussion

Some readers will want to use the stories in this book as a vehicle for self-exploration. The stories may in themselves trigger an association or a memory that then leads to new ideas or discoveries. Sometimes, a reader will want to take a story further, but will not know where to begin. These readers may appreciate the addition of the following questions that are not designed as homework, but merely intended as prompts to stimulate and guide one's thinking.

The questions, usually ten to twelve for each story, were generated by a group of nine readers who met several times to discuss the stories. Each reader brought a unique perspective to the discussion and offered one or two questions that coincided with a particular interpretation of the fable. As you read through the questions you may find a few that stimulate your own thinking in ways that you had not anticipated. Few, if any, readers will choose to answer all of the questions for a given story. If a question grabs you, let yourself play with it for a while in your head. Does the story still read the same way with this question in mind, or do you now see aspects of the story that you had overlooked before?

Some will want to answer the questions alone and in their heads. Others may want to keep a notebook and use the questions as part of a journal or diary. Still others will want to share the questions with a friend or with a counselor or therapist to help facilitate the formal process of self-exploration. Some may even want to use the stories and the accompanying questions to form the core of a discussion or support group. Any use of these questions, or no use at all, is just fine.

The Alchemist

1. If you were to design a healing formula for yourself, what would it be?

2. What are the necessary steps in the process of personal growth? Is there a step that eludes you?

3. When in your life have you waited for magic to happen? What was the outcome?

4. Is there a difference between that which is essential for your personal growth and those things you merely want or desire? Are they ever the same? How do you reconcile it when they are different?

5. Are there strengths you possess that you have overlooked or that may not be obvious?

6. Does it help you to believe in yourself if someone else expresses confidence in you? Have you ever "borrowed" someone else's enthusiasm?

7. Have you ever missed the trees because you have been so focused on the forest? Do you have goals that get in the way of enjoying everyday life?

8. Have there been times in your life when you were or felt tricked into doing something that was ultimately good for you? How did you feel about the trickery? Did the ends justify the means?

9. Are there people behind the scenes who are aiding or impeding your personal growth?

10. How is spirituality alive in your life? What aspects of your life have a spiritual dimension? Where is spirituality lacking?

Better Safe Than Sorry

1. How safe/anxious do you feel in the world?
2. Are you aware of ways in which you alter or limit your behavior because of fears? How have you adapted your life in order to feel safe?
3. How much do you think that your life is ruled by fear? What role does fear play in your decision-making process?
4. How do you draw the distinction between reasonable safety precautions and excessive fears that limit and define your existence?
5. How do we recognize when our efforts at self-protection are actually hurting us and impeding our efforts to get what we want?
6. When in your life have you gone through periods of heightened vulnerability? What caused you to feel at increased risk? What impact, if any, did media and community reports of violence have on your sense of personal safety?
7. What are your strategies for personal safety? Do any of those strategies result in isolation or cutting yourself off from things you enjoy?
8. What would you be willing to sacrifice in order to feel safe? Is there something you would never give up regardless of the risk involved?
9. Does safety necessarily mean that you must limit the way you live your life? Can you live life fully and still be safe? Can you go back and forth between safety and risk taking?
10. Are you aware of fears that plague you which seem not to burden others?
11. Do your limitations feel comfortable or do you want to find a way to live with more risk and perhaps more reward? Are there

times when you need to leave your fears behind and move on?

12. When you look back on your life, how would you like to say that you lived your life?

The Burden

1. Do you have a burden you carry? What is it? When did you become aware that you were carrying a burden? Did it seem unnecessary back then? Does it now?
2. Is it always clear what thing is a burden and what is not?
3. Is there an aspect of yourself for which you need to apologize? What is it?
4. Are there burdens that you may be able to put down temporarily? What is the difference between permanent and temporary relief from pain or distress?
5. What keeps you from freeing yourself from an unwanted burden?
6. Are there strengths or skills that become burdens? Might they become strengths again? How do you understand this transformation?
7. Do you think you might experience a sense of loss if you put a burden down? How would it be to face others free of your burden?
8. How do you react when people make you aware of a deficit or defect that you may have failed to notice?
9. What is the emotional space like in the time between realizing you are carrying a burden and putting it down? How do you manage your thoughts and feelings during that time?
10. How does recognizing a burden change the nature of the burden itself? Once you recognize a burden, does it cease to exist in the same way?

The Cave of Truth

1. How much (to what degree) does your truth need validation from others?

2. Have there been mentors or wise ones who have helped you in your personal growth? What role have they played?

3. How did you find the wise ones in your life? How did you know that they were worthy of trust?

4. Is there a cost to "borrowing wisdom" from someone else? Have you tried to use someone else's answers without success? What is the process of making someone else's wisdom your own?

5. Have you ever learned a truth that made you uncomfortable? How did you respond? How might you profitably incorporate uncomfortable truths into your life?

6. What role has disappointment played in your journey? How do you adjust to a path that seems blocked?

7. Is there an important role for "not having the answers?" Have you ever learned more by "not knowing?"

8. Can you go forward without knowing what lies ahead? What do you need in order to persist?

9. What are some of those things that you know to be true?

10. Do you have an inner "wise voice"? How did you come to know your intuitive self? Do you trust your own answers to important questions?

11. Is there a symbol, mark, or image that suggests your truth?

The Contest

1. Do you know what your own recipe for a happy life is?

2. Have you ever wished that someone else could tell you how to live in order to be happy?

3. If someone gave you their key to happiness would you take it readily or would you be reluctant to take someone else's solution?

4. Does a happy life mean that only good things happen to you or is it possible for a happy life to integrate events that are obviously stressful or sorrowful?

5. What is involved in being content? Is it different from feeling happy? How do you manage to feel content in the face of loss, sorrow, and distress?

6. How much does your perception of yourself influence your sense of being content?

7. How would you define a moment of pure bliss?

8. Is it ever possible that the same things that bring you joy also cause you unhappiness at times? On balance, how do you understand this paradox?

9. How can you balance having distant goals and being present in the moment? What happens when you focus so much on the "big happinesses" that you miss the everyday joys of living?

10. Is it possible to look at the experiences that you have had and to see them differently? What would it take to review your life and focus only on those things that have brought you pleasure?

11. Can you know joy if you have never experienced sorrow? How much are the down times an integral part of our appreciation of the good times?

12. Are there things or people in your life that you have failed to appreciate fully? What would it take to see them in a more positive light?

13. How much are our views of happiness determined by public perceptions of what constitutes the good life?

14. Think of someone whose life you have envied. Do you think they are as happy as you imagine? What might you be missing as you look at them and as you evaluate your own life?

15. How do you cultivate a positive view of yourself and your life when things are not going as you might wish?

16. Is there enough happiness to go around or does someone else's contentment lessen your own? How might another's contentment enhance your own?

The Diver

1. Is there a quality about yourself that you would like to change? Are there qualities that you do not possess that you would like to have?
2. What stops you from changing in ways that you would like?
3. What steps are there to accomplishing the goals that you have for yourself?
4 Do the changes that you want to make seem possible? Is hard work sufficient to get you where you want to go? Does change always require hard work?
5. How do you know when you are ready to take action or make a change?
6. When have you missed opportunities because you waited for someone else to give you permission to do what you already knew needed to be done?
7. What do you need in order to have enough faith in yourself to take action?
8. Are there people that you look to for guidance? What are they like and what do you need or expect from them as you try to change?
9. Even though you felt that it was time to move on, have you ever been reluctant to take necessary action? What things or feelings held you back? Do you know what you need to do in order to move forward?
10. What does it mean to have confidence in your own judgment?
11. What is the difference between being impulsive and foolhardy and trusting your own well thought out decisions?
12. When do you decide that the time has come to trust your

instincts versus the judgment of other people?

13. What is the basis of how you live your life? Are you more likely to follow internal or external guidance?

14. Do you have all the self-confidence that you would like? What needs to happen for you to believe in yourself more?

15. How can you begin to develop or trust an internal voice of encouragement so that you no longer need an outside guide to tell you what to do or how to behave?

The Gambler's Lesson

1. How do you evaluate the life you are living? What constitutes a "good hand" in life? Is it different for different people?

2. Have you ever felt that you were dealt a "bad hand?" How do you make the most of situations that on first blush do not seem positive?

3. Is there a way that you can take a "bad hand" and turn it to your advantage?

4. Are there circumstances in your life that keep you from moving forward? How do you control circumstances rather than letting them control you?

5. Have there been times in your life when you were better able to accomplish a goal without holding perfect cards? What characterized those times?

6. What skills do you need in order to make the most of life circumstances?

7. When you cannot control circumstances, how do you manage to tolerate the lack of control?

8. How do you present your cards in the best possible light?

9. What are you willing to do in order to create the changes that you want?

10. What does it mean to "win?" Do you know what you are trying to achieve?

11. If you do not like the rules of the games you are playing, is it possible to find a different game? Is it possible to modify the rules or change your perception of them? Are you ever tempted to find a way around the rules?

12. How does our culture define a winner? Do you assume that those who are successful have just gotten a better set of cards?

13. What role does luck play in your life?

The Gift of Choices

1. What decisions in your life seemed small but, in retrospect, had big implications? Are there choices that seemed big but, in retrospect, were not? How do we put choices in perspective?

2. If you were given a gift of choices, what "perfect decisions" would you make? Is there a current situation you wish you could solve in a "perfect" way?

3. What stops you from making decisions?

4. What do you need in order to make a choice? Think of your genie—what form would it take?

5. What have been the benefits of your choices over the years?

6. How do you know that you have made a good choice?

7. Think of a choice that was once good but now seems bad. Can you undo a choice?

8. When faced with choices, is it possible "not to decide"? How would it feel to take a pass on a particular decision?

9. What roles do wishing and hoping play in your decisions?

10. Are there opportunities you have missed because you failed to act?

11. What do you think remains in the silk bag at the end of the story? Do the contents have any value?

Gold and Silver

1. What is the relationship between responsibility and freedom in your life? Is it possible to balance responsibility and freedom or do they necessarily exist in opposition to one another?

2. What is the difference between concern and worry? What role does worry play in your life? How can you control your worry?

3. What are the varieties of love in your life? Are there different ways to love yourself? Other people? Activities in your life?

4. If you wanted to build more play or enjoyment into your life, how would you do it?

5. What are the areas of your life in which you feel you take good care of things? Are there changes that you want to make in how you care for things in your life? How much discipline does it take to make changes?

6. Has anyone given you a gift that influenced the course of your life? What was it and how did you take care of it?

7. Have there been people in your life who have seen your potential for growth and personal development? How did they show their faith in you?

8. Have there been people whose efforts have laid the groundwork for your own freedom or development? What did those people do that allowed you to follow your own path?

9. Is there something you feel you can dedicate yourself to? What would it take for you to achieve your very best?

10. If you could look back on your life and choose to have a more carefree or a more safe existence, which would you choose? What could you do now to make some of those changes possible?

11. What do you consider to be your life's work? What legacy might you want to pass on to the next generation?

Inktomi

1. Do you have trouble identifying your strengths or your personal beauty?
2. Is there some way in which you wish you were different?
3. What things have you "tried on" in response to feeling dissatisfied with yourself? With what results? At what cost?
4. Have you ever felt that you were willing to make changes at any cost? How impulse-driven do you think your desire for change is?
5. When someone offers you help, how quick are you to accept without thinking about what the consequences might be?
6. Do you find that you compare yourself to others? How does this interfere with your ability to see your own beauty?
7. Have you ever considered the role of self-hate in your life? Has it ever gotten to the point where it consumed you and threatened your existence?
8. Have you ever searched for something better only to find out that it was not what you expected?
9. What role do you think searching for something better plays in accepting who you are? Does it get in the way? Does it help you to see your own attributes more clearly?
10. What parts of yourself do you want to change? Are there parts of yourself that require a loving acceptance?
11. Have you come to accept parts of yourself that you once thought you needed to change?
12. Can you identify an element of hidden beauty that you do not usually acknowledge about yourself? Is there someone in your life who sees parts of you that you are prone to overlook?

Just One String

1. What are the essential things that define who you are?
2. Are there things that you feel you have lost as a result of your

experiences that make you feel less than whole?

3. If you lose something that defines who you are, how do you maintain your sense of integrity and meaning?

4. Is there any one thing whose loss would leave you feeling like a "different" person?

5. What are the unacceptable parts of who you are? Are there some aspects of yourself that you feel split off from? Is it necessary to learn to accept these parts of yourself or can they be discarded?

6. What role does memory play in defining who you are? How do you use your memories? Are they a hindrance or an asset in the process of moving forward?

7. How do you understand your sources of inner strength? How do you tap those sources during times of struggle?

8. What are the strategies you use to record your important memories?

9. Are there ways in which recording an experience keeps you from being present in the moment?

10. Are there people who have helped you to fill in the missing pieces in your life? How have they done this?

11. Are there memories you would like to recapture and hold on to? What would it take to make this happen? How might you respond if the experience seemed gone for good?

12. How do you take one important thread and make it part of a larger quilt?

13. What role does ritual play in your life? Are there traditions that make you feel part of something larger than yourself? How do you maintain connection to those rituals?

14. Think about creating your own Life Line. What would you include? Are there things you would want to leave out? Is there some benefit to recording both the good and the bad equally?

A Language of Your Own

1. How would you describe your own unique voice?

2. Have you ever given up your unique voice? What caused you to turn away from your own truth? What do you think would tempt you to give up your voice?

3. Have you ever felt that you could not make yourself understood? How did you handle that experience?

4. Have you ever had difficulty understanding the real meaning of what others were saying?

5. How do you communicate from the heart? Do you necessarily need words to do this?

6. How similar do we have to be in order to truly understand one another?

7. Is sameness a necessary virtue in a relationship? Do we understand each other better when we are the same? When we allow one another to be different?

8. Can you be connected to another person and still maintain your own individuality? How are similarity and connection related?

9. Are there some differences that make it impossible to communicate with another person? How do you judge when a difference is an impossible barrier?

10. When have you chosen to stop communication? What made you believe that it was hopeless to try and keep a dialogue open?

11. Have you ever struggled to communicate and ultimately achieved success? What strategies did you use to keep going?

12. What prompts you to communicate or act when it seems hopeless? What is the outcome of your continued trying? What role does your inner voice play in helping you to transcend silence?

13. What role does trust play in the ability to hear another person? How do you develop the necessary trust to allow communication to take place?

The Most Evil Man in Town

1. Have you become the person you thought you would be? How have life circumstances affected the way you have defined your life and who you have become?

2. How much control do you think we each have over the person we ultimately become?

3. What can you do if you find that your experience has changed you in ways that you do not like?

4. How is it possible for someone to change from being a gentle soul to being someone with a hard edge? Is there any going back?

5. Is it possible to live with an abuser and not take on some of the hard edge? How do you think it is possible to resist the negative influences?

6. Are we all really just a product of the environment we live in? What are the qualities of your environment that you value? What are the attributes you wish you could be rid of?

7. How do you respond when you feel that you have to make the best of a bad situation?

8. Do you ever find yourself doing things that you promised you would never do? How do you make sense of your behavior?

9. Is it possible to have power and only use it in charitable ways? Or does power always change us into someone willing to dominate others?

10. What is the difference between the power that makes us stronger and better people and the power that causes us to damage or hurt others?

11. What responsibility does each individual have for breaking the patterns of abuse and violence?

12. How do you find mentors or resources that pose an alternative to an abusive way of living if all you have ever known is violence and victimization?

The Options Trader

1. How do you define success? Do you know how to achieve it? What holds you back?
2. Are there things that you need to let go of in order to be successful?
3. How do you go through life? Are you always searching, never certain as to what the right path is, or do you act decisively?
4. When you do make choices, what are those variables that cause you to select one option over another?
5. Have there been times in your life when you have missed out on opportunities because you have been too fearful about actually making a choice?
6. Just because you make a particular choice does it necessarily mean that you cannot make other choices at some time in the future?
7. What is to be gained from committing yourself to one path over another? What are the advantages to waiting on the sidelines? How do you know which approach makes the most sense?
8. What is the cost of having multiple options? Is it possible to have too much freedom? Too many choices?
9. If your focus is too narrow, you may miss out on many life experiences. What do you feel that you are currently missing out on in your life? Is any of that due to an unwillingness to let go of unused possibilities?
10. Are there choices that you have made, or failed to make, that leave you feeling regretful? Are you more likely to regret decisions you made or decisions you failed to make?
11. Do you ever imagine that you will be without any options? What does that mean, to have "no options"?
12. How do you create options for yourself when you feel that your choices are limited? What constitutes a "good enough" option?
13. How do you make the most of a missed opportunity?

Perfect Vision

1. How do you define your own intuition? What is the difference between intuition and decision making that is based on fear and anxiety?

2. Have there been lessons that you learned from the experience or "vision" of others? What lessons have you had to learn from personal experience? What are the essential differences between these two ways of learning?

3. What keeps you from seeing the obvious outcome of certain behaviors or choices?

4. Have there been times when you saw something and did not tell others what you saw? Are there some truths that should not be spoken?

5. How do you convey concern and care without alienating the person you want to help? Do you have talents that might help those you care for without being too intrusive?

6. Can you receive warnings from others? What conditions make you able or unable to receive difficult communication?

7. When do you feel that you have an obligation to tell someone what you see despite what they might say or do?

8. How often are you correct in your assessment of how others will receive your advice?

9. Is there a price that you pay for speaking a truth that others may not want to hear? How much is isolation a part of that price?

10. Are there times when your vision is more the product of prejudice than wisdom?

11. How do you manage your own feelings when you have done all you can and still have no control over the outcome of events?

12. How much are uncertainty and anxiety a part of everyday life?

13. How much do you have to ignore everyday dangers in order to get on with the business of living your life? At what times

have you found it hard to wear necessary blinders?

14. What are the benefits of seeing and telling it like it is? How does your world change when you make a commitment to speak the truth?

The Pot of Misery

1. Do you have a pot of misery? Is it a person, place, or thing? Does it work for you the way it does for the girl in the story?

2. What strategies have you used to contain memories, sorrows, and other sources of pain? Which strategies have been particularly effective? Which have worked less well?

3. How often do you feel that it is necessary to revisit your sorrows? How is this revisiting helpful or not helpful?

4. Is there a pattern to how, when, and why you revisit the despair in your life? Do you actively decide when you are going to revisit past sorrows or does it just happen? What are the circumstances that trigger a revisitation?

5. What are you hoping will come of remembering the sorrow in your life? Are there lessons you want to learn or feelings you want to experience?

6. What happens when you accept that the past does not go away? Where are you in the process of acceptance?

7. What interferes with your being able to let go of past unhappiness?

8. Are there memories or feelings that you still long to let go? What do you think it would take to put those feelings or memories aside safely?

9. Have you ever felt that your pain was too much a part of you to let go? What do you have to lose if you let go of suffering?

10. Does misery really love company or do you need to be alone when you are feeling pain?

11. How do you allow other people to support you? Are there

ways in which you resist that support?

12. Is there a ritual that you can create for yourself to help put feelings of despair aside? How do you create enough space so that you can feel what you need to feel?

The Puzzler

1. What are the advantages in not remembering or not knowing some things about yourself and your past?

2. Are there missing parts of your story that you are still trying to piece together? Do you have any doubts about whether or not proceeding is a good idea?

3. What do you think would happen if you saw the entire puzzle all at once, not piece by piece? How might you react?

4. Why do you want more information about your history? How do you think life will change if you have more knowledge about your past?

5. Have you had warnings—either from others or from yourself— that you are treading on dangerous ground? Do you listen to those warnings? If not, why not?

6. What safeguards do you need to have in place as you embark on a journey of self-discovery? Are there ways you might prepare yourself beforehand?

7. Have you ever learned things that you wish you had left undiscovered? How did you cope with what you learned?

8. Can you create a story with the information that you do know and still be okay?

9. How do you avoid having painful knowledge define who you are? How can you put what you know into a healthy perspective?

10. What is necessary in order for you to accept yourself and the experiences that have shaped your personality?

Roots for Tanya

1. Think about an experience that required waiting. What was it like? What did you do to help yourself with the wait?

2. How do you experience impatience? What are you impatient about? What do you do when you are impatient?

3. How do you sit with your anxiety when you do not know what the outcome will be?

4. Which people have helped you to be more patient? What did they do to make the waiting easier? Did they share any advice or personal wisdom?

5. Has the process of healing or personal growth gone more slowly than you had expected or hoped?

6. How do you make sense of or understand the pace of your own internal process?

7. Does growth occur all at once or in increments? Can you notice the increments if all you focus on is the ultimate change?

8. How do you experience the small changes that constitute personal growth?

9. What kind of care do you need to give yourself during the process of personal growth?

10. Is there preparatory work you need to do before you begin the process of personal growth?

11. How do you reward yourself for the progress you have made?

12. When does too much concern or focus get in the way of accomplishing your goal?

13. How long has it taken for real change to take root in your life? Are there some changes that seem to grow quickly once they are established? Are there others that progress slowly even when they are well rooted?

The Silver Flute

1. When you first began a process of personal growth, change, or recovery, what did you think the journey would be like? How long did you think the process would take?
2. What does it mean to be "motivated" to change?
3. Think of the difference between a goal and the process of reaching that goal. Do you have goals for which you can/cannot find a path to success?
4. Are there strategies that worked in the past to achieve goals that no longer seem adequate?
5. What keeps you from investing energy in yourself?
6. If hard work is your "last alternative," what are the "easy" strategies for getting what you want?
7. Are there times when you fool yourself while you are trying to fool someone else?
8. Are there some areas of your life for which success seems easier/harder than others?
9. What are the advantages to hard work? Is there any value in suffering? What do you think it might be?
10. What qualities does it take to be the "ruler" of your own life? How do you attain those?

Speak to Me

1. Have you lost loved ones? Do you still feel a connection to them? What is that connection like?
2. How can you keep the memory of people who have died or moved on? What strategies do you use to keep memories fresh?
3. Who are the special people in your life? Do you ever find yourself saying or doing things in a way that reminds you of these special people? How do you feel when you become aware of the connection?

4. What personal qualities have you inherited that you want to keep and what personal qualities do you feel have became a burden? Is there a way in which you might let go of some of those attributes that trouble you?

5. How do you react when you find yourself doing something that you did not like in someone else?

6. Were you ever told that you were just like someone else? Did that observation give you comfort or was it disturbing?

7. Are there personal qualities that you have inherited that you can use in a positive way even if those attributes are objectively negative?

8. What are the traditions, customs, or bits of wisdom that have been passed on to you that you would like to pass on to the next generation?

9. Are there people in your life now with whom you would like to build closer connections? What might you do to strengthen those connections?

10. What rituals can you establish for yourself that might allow you to maintain contact with people who have passed on?

11. How might you use meditation or prayer to feel close to those who have passed on?

The Travelers

1. Do you know what brings you happiness?

2. Do you long for something else that you feel will make you happy? Do you know what it is? How will you recognize it when it comes?

3. How do you find people who share your vision of happiness?

4. How much deviation from your ideal are you willing to accept? Can you imagine a range of different options any one of which might make you happy?

5. How much does your happiness come from the outside? The

inside? Can you embrace your life when externals are not going your way?

6. How do you manage those days that are not "perfect"? How hard is it to accept that some days are "just okay"?

7. How do you take time each day to notice the simple joys and pleasures?

8. Have you had experiences with friends or loved ones where you disagreed about what mattered? How did you manage to keep those differences in perspective?

9. Have you ever made decisions or choices based on someone else's notion of the "good life"? What was the cost?

10. How often do you feel envious or jealous of others? What things cause you to feel envious or jealous? How do you manage those feelings?

11. What elements of your current life do you want to hold on to? What elements do you want to change? What steps do you need to take to create the life you want?

12. When you do not have the life you might want for yourself, how do you maintain inner harmony? What steps do you take to feel at peace? Does faith or spirituality play a part?

The Twenty-Four Carat Buddha

1. How do you know when something or someone is authentic?

2. Have you ever mistaken a fake for the genuine article? Have you ever thought the "real thing" was just another counterfeit?

3. What evidence do you ignore in a new relationship, a new job, or a new opportunity? Are there consequences to not seeing?

4. What are your vulnerabilities? If you were to be seduced, how would someone hook you in?

5. What environments or situations, exotic or otherwise, lead you to give away some of your power and behave more naively?

6. Have you ever presented yourself as other than you really are? What were your motives? How did you feel about duping someone?

7. Have you ever had your enthusiasm or your dreams dashed by others? How did you respond? What helped you maintain hope or a vision of something better?

8. For how long do you hold onto your dreams when evidence to the contrary exists? What does it mean to "face reality"?

9. How do you think the girl in the story responded to the feedback from her friends? Would she have been happier believing in the genuineness of her Buddha?

10. How much honesty do you want from your friends? Loved ones? Colleagues?

Two Gifts

1. Have there been times when you have worn rose-colored glasses? Why? And for how long?

2. How or why did the glasses come off? Did someone else or some external circumstance play a role?

3. Have other people encouraged you to keep the glasses on? What was their agenda?

4. Have you felt that different gifts, qualities, or virtues have been important at different times in your life? Is change a process with a natural order that cannot or should not be violated?

5. What constitutes a "full life"? How does it differ from a "problem-free" life?

6. How often do you dismiss good advice because it is not exactly what you want to hear?

7. How bad do things have to get for you to embrace the advice that others give you? Do you ever accept it willingly? Or do you have to awaken to the truth on your own?

8. What is your personal truth? Have you been able to see it clearly?

9. Have you ever had to balance competing truths in your life?

10. Who do you want to share your truth with? Should it be public? Are there times when it makes sense to keep the truth private?

11. What challenges do you face? Can you see a positive outcome? What do you think it will take to bring about a triumph?

The Wizard's Message

1. Do you have a mantra that has guided your actions or helped you to survive through difficult times?

2. Is there a guiding principle that you could adopt that would help you to have a more fulfilling life? Is there a goal or a dream that you would like to pursue but do not have the right guiding principle for?

3. Is there a difference between thinking positively and being naive and unrealistic about what is possible? Have you ever found yourself ignoring important information?

4. Where do your principles come from? Are they shared by others?

5. Can you have a single principle that guides your entire life? Have you used different pieces of wisdom for different times in your life?

6. Have you ever found yourself too attached to a principle?

7. Have you ever found yourself on a quest that seemed futile? How do you know when it is time to change the quest and set off on another path?

8. How much choice do you feel you have in your life? Do you feel attached to old beliefs that have outlived their usefulness?

9. What risks are you willing to take in order to get what you want? Are there some risks not worth taking? What are they?

10. When do you feel that you have enough and striving after more is unnecessary?

11. Are there times when you have pushed yourself too hard? How do you know when to back off?

12. Have you ever lost sight of what your true goals were? What caused you to lose your vision? Are there personal goals that you know you need to pursue?

13. If things do not work out as you hope, how do you prevent the outcome from being devastating? What do you do when the pursuit causes you pain and distress? Do you continue a difficult quest or do you give up and turn your attention elsewhere?

14. Are there new mantras that you might now create for yourself?

About the Sidran Institute

**The Sidran Institute, a leader in traumatic stress educa-
tion and advocacy,** is a nationally focused nonprofit organ-
ization devoted to helping people who have experienced
traumatic life events. Our education and advocacy promotes
greater understanding of:

- The early recognition and treatment of trauma-related
  stress in children;
- The understanding of trauma and its long-term effect
  on adults;
- The strategies leading to greatest success in self-help
  recovery for trauma survivors;
- The clinical methods and practices leading to greatest
  success in aiding trauma victims;
- The development of public policy initiatives that are
  responsive to the needs of adult and child survivors of
  traumatic events.

To further this mission, Sidran operates the following programs:

The Sidran Institute Press publishes books and educational
materials on traumatic stress and dissociative conditions. A
recently published example is *Growing Beyond Survival:
A Self-Help Toolkit for Managing Traumatic Stress,* by
Elizabeth Vermilyea. This innovative workbook provides
skill-building tools to empower survivors to take control of
their trauma symptoms.

Some of our other titles include *Risking Connection: A Training Curriculum for Working with Survivors of*

Childhood Abuse (a curriculum for mental health professionals and parapro-fessionals), *Managing Traumatic Stress Through Art* (an interactive work-book to promote healing), and *Understanding the Effects of Traumatic Stress* (a manual for community agencies).

The Sidran Bookshelf on Trauma and Dissociation is an annotated mail order and web catalog of the best in clinical, educational, and survivor-sup-portive literature on post-traumatic stress, dissociative conditions, and relat-ed topics.

The Sidran Resource Center—drawing from Sidran's extensive database and library—provides resources and referrals at no cost to callers from around the English-speaking world. The referral database includes: trauma-experienced therapists, traumatic stress organizations, educational books and materials, conferences, trainings, and treatment facilities.

Sidran Education and Training Services provide conference speakers, pre-programmed and custom workshops, consultation, and technical assistance on all aspects of traumatic stress including:

- **Agency Training** on trauma-related topics, such as Trauma Symptom Management, Assessment and Treatment Planning, Borderline Person-ality Disorder, and others. We will be glad to customize presentations for the specific needs of your agency.
- **Survivor Education** programming including how to start and main-tain effective peer support groups, community networking for trauma support, successful selection of therapists, coping skills, and healing skills.
- **Public Education** workshops on understanding PTSD and the psycho-logical outcomes of severe childhood trauma for a variety of audiences: adult survivors, partners and supporters, caregivers of abused children, and nonclinical professionals (such as teachers, social services person-nel, clergy, etc.).

For more information on any of these programs and projects, please contact us:

The Sidran Institute
200 East Joppa Road, Suite 207, Baltimore, MD 21286
Phone: 410-825-8888 • Fax: 410-337-0747
E-mail: help@sidran.org • Website: www.sidran.org

About the Author

Maxine Harris, Ph.D., is a clinical psychologist and the co-director and cofounder of Community Connections, the largest full-service nonprofit community mental health agency in Washington, D.C. She also has an active private psychotherapy practice and has published several books and numerous articles on various topics including grief and loss, trauma recovery, and the nexus between myth and psychotherapy.